Lighting the Fuse

Lighting the Fuse

Stories from Britain's first
female bomb disposal expert

Lucy Lewis

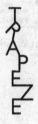

First published in Great Britain in 2021 by Trapeze
This paperback edition published in 2022 by Trapeze,
an imprint of The Orion Publishing Group Ltd
Carmelite House, 50 Victoria Embankment
London EC4Y 0DZ

An Hachette UK Company

1 3 5 7 9 10 8 6 4 2

A CIP catalogue record for this book
is available from the British Library.

ISBN (Paperback) 978 1 8418 8394 6
ISBN (eBook) 978 1 8418 8395 3
ISBN (Audio) 978 1 8418 8398 4

Typeset by Input Data Services Ltd, Somerset

Printed and bound in Great Britain by Clays Ltd, Elcograf S.p.A.

MIX
Paper from
responsible sources
FSC® C104740

www.orionbooks.co.uk

To the three bravest of women:
my mother, my sister and my daughter.

Contents

Author's Note

This book is based on my diaries, records and recollection of events. The following names are pseudonyms: Corporal Gregg, Jane, Ken, Captain Wallis, Staff Sergeant Beech, Captain Flatley, Colonel Knight, Miss Morton, Ben, Jackie, David, Graham, Roger, JJ, Bob, Mark, Tennison, Thompson, Newman, Taylor, Corporal Thorpe and Fred.

In Memoriam

Captain Lisa Head

Killed defusing an IED in Afghanistan 19 April 2011

Aged 29

'I fear there is a complex against women being connected with lethal work. We must get rid of this.'

Prime Minister Winston Churchill to his Secretary of State for War, 1941

Prologue

'This could be it,' I mutter to myself, as I try in vain to make out the faces of the people on the pavement, all just a blur by the time we've reached and swept past them. The buildings we whizz past blend into one amorphous block. I am in the passenger seat of a speeding Land Rover, its blue lights flashing as we try to keep pace with the police escort up ahead. I cast a sideways glance at the driver, Corporal Gregg, whose eyes are bright with excitement. He bites his moustached top lip and grips the swinging wheel for dear life as he just about keeps the wallowing hippo of a vehicle in the middle of the narrow Kent road. Our Land Rover is heavily laden and rolls perilously on the corners. I cautiously glance back to check the kit stowed behind us; we are carrying boxes of sensitive detonators but also enough plastic explosive to practically vaporise us. The hairs on the back of my neck prick up in nervous anticipation as my lunch begins to make itself known in the pit of my stomach. I'm starting to feel nauseous – I hate being car-sick.

I am twenty-six years old, a Duty Bomb Disposal Officer, the first woman ever to be listed on the Operational

Bomb Disposal Officer Roster and this is my very first emergency call-out. We are on our way to investigate the report of a bomb found when a homeowner was digging in his garden on a newly built housing estate, trying to set out the flower beds.

Corporal Gregg glances over at me. I have worked with him before but only in the relative calm of the Regimental Headquarters, where he is one of my troop of clerks. I trust him completely but I don't want to give anyone the chance to tell the story of the vomiting female bomb disposal officer. There are plenty of men who still think the high pressure, high stakes world of bomb disposal is no place for a woman. It's one extra distraction I have to get out of my mind if I am going to focus on the job ahead. Not for the first time I think of the old Ginger Rogers adage, that she had to be able to do everything Fred Astaire did but backwards *and* in heels.

Luckily Corporal Gregg is clearly enjoying himself too much to notice my nervousness. As we hurtle through the countryside in the wake of the police car, he hauls us around a roundabout. The opposing traffic has pulled over to let us pass. All they see is a large white Land Rover flash past with its front wings painted red. No one remembers that the red wings were the wartime equivalent of blue lights when the blackout didn't allow lights at all – and for fifty years they have put out the same message: 'Let us through,' they scream, 'there's a bomb we need to make safe.'

I grit my teeth, trying to focus on the task ahead and resisting the temptation to hang on to the grab handle above the passenger door. As well as the nervousness, a bigger part of me is alive and buzzing with the excitement of possibility – this could be it! My big World War II German iron bomb! The type every Royal Engineers bomb disposal officer longs to be called to. This is what all the training was for: all those hours spent practising drilling into bomb fuzes, learning to wire up explosive charges and examining suspicious rusting lumps of metal. When we arrive at the bomb all eyes will look to me for guidance. I'll be making decisions that are the difference between life and death. Ever since the beginning of the Blitz in 1940 it has always been men who set off to deal with the unexploded bombs and munitions that war leaves behind, with little protection against the danger. Today, for the first time ever, it will be a woman – me. No pressure.

A few hours earlier I had been spending a quiet Sunday afternoon ironing my kit, a classic military pastime, and checking my duty pager every few minutes. I wasn't nervous so much as expectant, as if I suspected what the day would hold.

Right now, as I'm flung sideways against the door, it's like being on the fairground waltzers and we're gaining on the police escort that is guiding us to our target. As we race through the empty Dartford Tunnel all traffic is stopped, because live explosives aren't allowed to share the confined space with other vehicles. Not for the first time I think about the route that has brought me here, to this point.

'We're getting close.'

I nod. This is it.

I

Brave New World

Sometimes what happens in life comes down to whether you are prepared to eat the raw hedgehog or not.

It's three years before I'm sitting in the wailing Land Rover alongside Corporal Gregg and I'm aiming to be selected to join Operation Raleigh, a development charity which aims to inspire young people to make a positive impact in the world. Jane and Ken, the two laid-back twenty-something former Operation Raleigh Venturers leading us would-be Venturers, look down at the remains of the half-cooked hedgehog and then up at me. Their meaning is horribly clear. I feel it wise to clarify the situation so there is no misunderstanding.

'If I eat that, then I pass?' Grins and nods all round.

The charity's mission is to send young Venturers aged between eighteen and twenty-four to far-flung corners of the globe so they can help local communities and return with life skills to assist people in their own country. One of the options is to join the crew of a tall ship sailing around South America, up the Amazon and into the Caribbean, monitoring sea life and water quality. That sounded much more exciting than digging a well in Chile, so I put my name down for the ship.

Before I can get there though, I have to spend the last couple of days stomping about in the grounds of Welbeck, the military sixth form college, failing to impress in a variety of stamina, raft-building and map-reading exercises. On the final day, after a brief demonstration, we are required to make a campfire and then cook and eat a meal based on a dead animal, plus whatever we can forage. After a long weekend of draining activity I am so hungry that even a dried-up old tea bag from the car park bin is looking tasty. My small group is allocated a dead chicken to pluck and cook, along with some tatty vegetables, so we divide up the tasks and set to work lighting a fire and picking nettles for our nettle tea. A dead hedgehog has just been discovered in the car park and Jane and Ken are demonstrating how it can be cooked by baking it in clay. We need to be prepared to eat whatever is on offer in whichever remote corner of the world we may find ourselves. I think my group do quite well but Ken inspects our progress and announces that it is not substantial enough and we need more nettles.

As I wander out into the bushes, I wonder what I'm doing here. I only applied for this because my employer had sponsored the selection weekend and I wanted to show that I was keen for promotion. I hadn't considered that I might actually pass these demanding tests and now that I am here I really, really want to succeed and my hitherto dormant sense of adventure is suddenly awakened. As I trudge along wearing a numbered bib I realise that I've been missing out by playing it safe with a decent, steady job in airport security. I need to try something else before

I end up joining in with my older colleagues, who are constantly moaning about pensions and retirement planning. First of all, I want to truly live. I can see the long familiar road of career and family stretching out ahead of me, as it did for so many women of my age, and I decide I want to try something else first.

By the time I return with armfuls of nettles, the other candidates have eaten the cooked outer hedgehog and all that is left are the raw bits in the middle. I close my eyes, push the wet, pink blob into my mouth, hold my breath so I can't taste it, chew briefly and swallow fast. Little did I realise that by making this bizarre, seemingly insignificant choice, I was setting myself on a path that would have me pushing my personal boundaries and rising to the challenges I was faced with for the rest of my career.

Thankfully the hedgehog did me no physical harm (although the fact that I can still remember it suggests that maybe it's had a lasting mental impact) and I passed the Operation Raleigh selection process. Six months later I found myself on board a tall ship, the brigantine *Zebu*, which I would call home for the next three months as she sailed from Salvador in Brazil to Belém, the gateway to the Amazon, and went island-hopping, finishing her two-year round-the-world voyage in Antigua. Our crew was small, just sixteen Venturers like me, guided by a professional crew of six.

I felt seasick immediately after setting sail from Salvador. And so the nightmare began. After two days at sea – while everyone else had gained their sea legs – I was at death's door, lying spread-eagled on the deck day and night, only moving to crawl to the leeward rail to be sick or to find some kind of shelter from the baking sun and tropical rain. Dysentery then added to my misery. I tried to eat every meal but Mouthful Number Two would meet Mouthful Number One going the other way. After twenty minutes of failing to get the same cold, soggy, bile mush to stay inside my body I would give up. By Day Four, not only was nothing staying down but I was also too weak to crawl out of the sun and my eyelids were so badly blistered it felt like agony. I wasn't sure how much more I could take. By the sixth day at sea I had had enough: my hips were badly bruised and my joints were sore from lying on the hard-rolling deck all week. Life had reached an all-time low. I had to be tied to the leeward rail as I was not strong enough to hold on by myself and I was not even cheered up by watching the dolphins follow the ship – their long, silvery shadows visible under the water at night. I dread to think how much weight I lost during the truly most miserable week of my life. I looked like a burnt matchstick with all my strength and fitness gone and I wasn't sure how much longer I could carry on.

Rescue from this waking nightmare came in the shape of an island, Fernando de Noronha, some 220 miles off the Brazilian coast. Never had a sight been more welcome. After a few days of respite at anchor, while I gained strength, we set sail once more, stopping at the Amazonian port of Belém before departing on the evening tide towards Devil's Island and French Guiana.

One evening, about two hours after sunset and hundreds of miles offshore, I'm lying below decks on my narrow bunk feeling nauseous as usual. All I can hear is

Venturer Pete the Pilot's gentle snore and the splatter of rain overhead. Other Venturers Malaria Matthew, Aussie Lindy and Ski Instructor Sue are playing cards quietly in the saloon next door. Suddenly we hear a piercing scream.

'Man overboard! Man overboard!'

There's a crash from the saloon as the card players hurl themselves towards the steep companionway that leads to the deck. My heart thumping I launch from my bunk, getting my feet on the stairs seconds before Pete does. Someone is ringing the ship's bell continually to sound the alarm, increasing the sense of urgency. It has only taken seconds for everyone to get on deck. The watch, who were sailing the ship at the time, have already thrown both safety flares overboard to mark the location where someone was lost. The life rings have also been flung behind the ship for a swimmer to cling to if they were heading for the flares. Skipper Pete (yes, there were two Petes aboard our boat) is at the helm, holding a straight course so the small inflatable boat, kept on board for emergencies such as these, can head directly astern in the right direction. The ringing bell also helps to indicate our location in the dark, giving the swimmer a target to aim for when all they can see around them are walls of dark water.

We all know what to do because we've practised this before, but only in good weather and in daylight – never in the semi-darkness of a three-quarter moon on a rainy night in heavy seas. We are desperate to stop the ship from sailing away from the spot where the person went over. Ships have no brakes so we rip down the sails to reduce her speed. She is under full sail and every inch of canvas is pulling us further away from someone fighting for their life in the churning sea. Their only hope is that we can slow down enough to be in range when the little inflatable boat is launched to go back and search the rolling swell for the dark dot of a human head above the water.

Who is it? Who's missing? I lock eyes with Lindy and our hands touch briefly as we both try to grip the wet rope to haul the huge mainsail onto the deck. The rescue boat cannot be launched while the sail is up. Venturers heave at the tarpaulin that covers the small inflatable boat, muscles straining to pull the soaking cover away from the one thing that could save our shipmate. The moment the heavy sail is down Venturers grapple with the harness that enables the inflatable to be lifted off the deck. The bosun, Tony, leaps up into the swaying rigging to release the hook and the instant that hook meets harness the cry goes out: 'Haul away! Haul away!'

Fear and worry still show on all our faces as the boat is swung over the leeward rail. A searchlight skips the surface of the heaving water and finds the bobbing flares before they disappear behind a wave. Skipper Pete steers into the wind in order to slow *Zebu* down yet further and Venturer Rob and crewman Kev quickly don lifejackets, grabbing a spare for the victim before scrambling down into the inflatable. The engine roars and they speed away towards the flares, but are quickly lost behind the towering waves. With the immediate rush over there is nothing more we can do but keep watch and wait. Breathless from our exertions and stunned by the shock of it all, we ask who has gone overboard and what happened.

As we catch our breath, Bob, one of the American

Venturers, explains what had happened just five minutes earlier. He and Steve, a British Venturer, had been stowing the sails on the bowsprit, he said, when: 'The footrope that Steve was standing on suddenly snapped and dropped him, like a stone, into the bow-wave. I couldn't do anything to help except shout the alarm.'

The next twenty minutes are agonising as we sit and wait, but thankfully we see the lights of the lifeboat drawing closer with a clearly shaken, and very wet, Steve sitting aboard. There is no real celebration, just a huge sigh of relief and nightmares all round as we now have no smoke flares or life rings left. Without them even daytime rescue is nigh impossible.

As soon as we've all recovered from the drama, Steve tells us that after he fell into the water the ship then sailed straight over him, pushing him under the shallow hull. He surfaced behind the stern and watched it sail away into the inky night. Luckily for him the propeller had not been turning so his only injuries were scrapes from the underside of the hull. He acted quickly by diving under the water to wrestle his waterproof jacket off and then made a float with it to keep his head above water. Looking for the ship in the dark was hopeless but as the swell lifted him he caught sight of the black outline of *Zebu* turning into the wind. Being a strong swimmer he started to head for the ship, then above the sounds of the sea he heard the engine of the inflatable boat and screamed 'Over here!', while waving frantically. The little boat came alongside him, Rob and Kev hauled him aboard and he is back on *Zebu*'s pitching deck just twenty-one minutes after the footrope snapped.

I zone out for a couple of moments, letting my mind wander back to the safety of the airport and the job I left to take part in Operation Raleigh. I can't help but think that my work there now seems very monotonous and flat. At first, I had naively assumed that I would gradually adjust to normal living once this adventure was over but something is telling me that I wouldn't, couldn't, settle back into my previous existence – I would never be able to get through another twelve-hour shift. I'd loved the job for years before Operation Raleigh came along but I am fast losing interest, so returning to that life is out of the question. I'm jolted out of my thoughts by Lindy, who elbows me and nods towards Skipper Pete just as he says: 'In all my years at sea, Steve is the first person I've ever known be found alive after dark.'*

Two years later, it's the second day of the year and although I'm still recovering from a joint New Year's Eve and leaving party, I'm off to Sandhurst to join the Army. The previous night I was so hungover that I had to phone my mother to come help me carry my bags down the stairs. Perhaps not the ideal preparation for what will be one of the hardest physical and mental challenges of my life. I'm off to start a totally new life equipped only with a pasty tinge and an ironing board.†

* *Operation Raleigh – Adventure Unlimited*, John Blashford-Snell, 1990, HarperCollins.
† It was the first of seven ironing boards. The Army is nothing if not passionate about the competitive sport that is ironing. I haven't really described how much ironing is involved but the fact that the first day of Sandhurst is called 'Ironing Board Sunday' tells you all you need to know.

After driving for an hour and a half, Sandhurst's red-edged sign creeps into view. 'Royal Military Academy.' The words make the butterflies in my stomach morph into nausea. *What have I done? I've given up a well-paid, secure job and rented out my house and here I am on the doorstep of the world's premier military academy for officers, with no real idea of what happens next. What was I thinking?* My little car seems to drive itself towards the formal, white-pillared facade of the small gatehouse, surrounded by austere black, gold-topped railings.

As I find out over the coming months of training, somewhere behind this lodge lies a complex of buildings similar to a university campus; library, gym, swimming pool, shop, classrooms, lecture halls, accommodation blocks, etc. Unlike a university, though, it is also equipped with assault courses, shooting ranges, gas chambers, stables, parade squares, a hospital, a chapel, a cemetery and a housing estate for the permanent staff. The extensive, immaculate grounds are also steeped in history, as they are spattered with large bronze statues, such as that of the Prince Imperial surrounded by bronze eagles,* massive mortars and weaponry that has been captured through the ages. All this I will soon discover as I run past these landmarks, lungs burning, trying to keep up with the racing snakes† on yet another timed run, each statue indicating how far to suffer till the finish line, but as I approach the formidable gate with its stripy barrier and metal skirt, I know nothing

---

* It was the Prince Imperial statue that months later Moira and I failed to climb on Red Nose Day, so Napoleon Bonaparte's great-nephew was saved the ignominy of wearing a plastic red nose.

† A racing snake is a very skinny person who is an extremely fast runner.

apart from the brief contents of the glossy Sandhurst brochure.

Back home, when I first flicked through the brochure, I was enthralled by the pictures of helmeted cadets on the assault course, marching in handsome blue uniforms on a gleaming parade square and running exhausted through a muddy stream carrying a telegraph pole. One of the details the brochure missed was that there are three colleges: Old College (the standard image of Sandhurst with its cream façade, Grand Entrance and captured Waterloo cannons); red-bricked mansion house New College and concrete Victory College. But perhaps more importantly, the brochure also failed to mention that while male cadets are split into numerous* companies, only two companies are made up of female cadets, who largely train separately from the men and have a slightly different syllabus – more paperwork, less trench digging.

As I draw near I'm still amazed that I got into Sandhurst at all. I never expected to pass the rigorous medical in the first place. When I was seventeen my wrist was crushed in a motorbike accident and as a souvenir my right hand is now twisted at the wrong angle as well as being out of line. The result is a weak right arm with limited movement in my crooked wrist. My simple solution to passing the medical was to wear a special yellow T-shirt. The sheaf of instructions for the medical appointment said to bring PE kit as the assessment would involve vigorous exercise, so based on its previous success on the Operation Raleigh

---

* There can be anything up to ten companies and their names change from year to year.

selection weekend I wear my bright yellow *Krypton Factor*[*]
T-shirt. I hope this will distract the doctor and create the
impression that I might be fit.

I am so nervous that I arrive an hour early and my
heart rate is still far too high by the time the appointment
begins. I have a chest X-ray and the usual blood pressure
and stethoscope stuff, so far so good, but then we move
on to the tricky bit I have been dreading – my crooked
and now arthritic arm. Arthritis set in only months after
the accident, when I was just eighteen. At first glance it
looks fine but compared to the left forearm it is obviously
deformed. This means that the bones of my forearm can't
cross over as the hand tries to rotate, so I have very limited
movement in any direction and have to use my shoulder
to compensate. I focus on persuading the doctor that I
should be allowed to join up. First of all, I demonstrate the
extent of the movement I do have and then explain that I
find it difficult to do gym exercises as my wrist won't bend
backwards far enough to put my hand flat on the floor
for a press-up. I can usually get round the problem and I
prove this by doing a press-up on my fingers, karate-style.
However, I don't mention that I can't do chin-ups at all as
the forearm is fixed – I just hang there, immobile, unable
to bend my arm even a fraction. There is a long pause as
he looks at me over his glasses.

'Did you actually go on the *Krypton Factor*?' he asks,
pointing at my T-shirt with his pen.

'Yes, I did.'

---

[*] *The Krypton Factor* was a challenging TV game show (1977–1995) that
tested 'superhuman' powers of physical stamina and mental agility; it fa-
mously featured a timed Army assault course.

'And how did you do on the assault course?'

'I was the second fastest woman in the series,' I reply truthfully, but completely failing to mention that I was last in my individual programme.

'Good, that's the hardest physical challenge your arm will have to cope with, so Sandhurst will just have to deal with the fact that you can't do certain gym exercises.'

And with that I am through!

My arm is not a major problem in ordinary civilian life but it becomes a real issue when I do anything adventurous. As soon as I joined the tall ship *Zebu* on Operation Raleigh the year before Sandhurst, and looked up at the swaying rigging high above me, I knew my injury would be put to the toughest of tests. Halfway up one of the masts was the crow's nest or platform and to reach it I had to briefly hang from a single handhold. I looked up at the overhang in dismay, not fully trusting the damaged wrist to hold my weight. I would have to lean back to grasp the rigging above with one hand and then pull up from hand to hand, my hands and arms bearing my full body weight while my legs dangle uselessly in the air underneath the platform. I watched with dread as the other Venturers scrabble for a handhold and I could see their arms straining with the effort of what was essentially a one-handed chin-up, high above the unforgiving deck.

Once I'd climbed up the tapering rigging as far as the platform underside I stopped to assess the situation, trying not to look down at the deck far beneath me: a fall from this height would be fatal. On my first attempt, I decided to hang from the crook of my elbow and clamber awkwardly up onto the platform. Once there, I sat down with my back against the mast, feet swinging free. I had done it! It wasn't fast or pretty but at least I'd achieved it somehow.

I was slightly more confident the second time aloft, although my inner elbow was so badly bruised from the first attempt that I quickly reverted to using my dodgy hand. I just had to hope that my wrist would support my bodyweight. By the end of the three-month expedition, I could hang by the fingertips of my crooked hand and I climbed the 85 feet from deck to masthead as easily as walking upstairs. It's all a matter of overcoming one's initial fear and self-doubt and then building up confidence.

Now, as I approach the Academy gates, I begin to realise that Sandhurst is going to test both my wrist and my confidence to the absolute limit.

My military experience to date is limited to just two weeks of basic soldier training a year ago with the Territorial Army (TA). It took place at the all-female WRAC* Centre in Guildford (where all female soldiers train). There I learned how to march, iron uniform and lace my boots correctly, but not much more. This introduction to military life was followed by a few weekends running around an assault course in between studying radio procedure and a bit more marching, which sums up my total practical knowledge. Like so many others, I enjoyed my experience

---

* Women's Royal Army Corps – pronounced W-R-A-C – the only part of the non-medical Army that women could join at the time. Women were administrators by 'trade' within the WRAC, although a sizeable number of my cohort were qualified teachers and would spend their careers permanently attached to the Royal Army Educational Corps, teaching promotion courses and general education with opportunities to become interpreters.

with the part-time TA and was convinced that joining the full-timers was my next step. Now I have taken the plunge to join the Regular Army I will have to learn a whole lot more – and fast – if I am ever to become an officer.

A stern-looking soldier in combat dress waves me to a parking bay, so I dutifully park as neatly as I can. I'm instructed to sign in and then I am directed towards the solid-pillared building beside the gate. The smell of floor polish hits me hard as I enter, so strong I can taste it in the back of my throat. I immediately feel queasy again. There is a bored-looking contractor in grubby overalls standing before the desk, clearly waiting for permission to enter. He looks very out of place in this shining palace of efficiency and control. I glance around me momentarily, taking in the noticeboard, which is like none that I have ever seen before. Notices are equidistant and perfectly aligned, with a drawing pin at each corner. Nothing is so much as a millimetre out of place, which I find rather unnerving.

The immaculately dressed soldier standing behind the huge desk looks me up and down and curtly instructs me to fill in a form, then a line in a book: date, time, name, unit (what's that?), car registration. I'm handed a sheaf of paperwork and given a few concise directions: past the statue, past the lake, Victory College on the right. Park first, then offload kit, move car to distant car park later. I walk back to my car, put the pass on the dashboard and quickly look at the map on the back, because I've forgotten everything after 'past the statue'. I resolve to pull over and have a proper look when I am not being watched.

After I crawl past numerous neat red signs I realise

that there is more than one sodding lake, but I eventually pull up at Victory College: a monstrosity of thick pebble-dashed slabs, pencil-thin windows and ghastly grey concrete blocks on concrete stilts – a truly ugly building. They don't put that one in the brochure so it's not what I expect, but who cares? I am here now. I step out of the car and drag my luggage from the boot. I've parked on an asphalt area about a hundred metres from the concrete stilts – I find out later that no vehicles are allowed any closer in case they contain a car bomb, a hint of the danger from terrorism that I will face throughout my entire military career. Heart thumping, I'm greeted by unsmiling people with shiny peaks and shiny shoes. On their upper arms they wear their badges of rank: three stripes with a crown above them. From my time with the Territorial Army I already know what they are: staff sergeants! Welcome to the Army.

A formidable slim woman with short, grey-flecked dark hair and a confident stride wields a clipboard with ruthless efficiency. In place of a watch on her wrist she wears a warrant officer's* brass crown on a leather strap – this is our Company† Sergeant Major (just one rank above but in reality a massive leap beyond the staff sergeants who first greeted me at Victory College). I instantly realise that I

---

* Warrant officers are highly specialised experts and trainers in their field. Junior soldiers call them Sir or Ma'am but don't salute them.

† Some parts of the Army, the Royal Engineers for example, have squadrons and some, such as the Royal Military Police, have companies. A company is a sub-unit of a regiment, with 120–200 soldiers commanded by a major. A platoon is a sub-division of a company. A troop is a sub-division of a squadron.

need to keep a very, very low profile if I am to escape her withering gaze and avoid being found wanting.

'Name?'

'Stephens,' I reply quickly, trying to mask the fact that I am out of breath after just carrying my luggage up one flight of stairs. My suitcases are weighed down by the exhaustive list of kit we must bring with us. Every course in the Army has a detailed kit list among the extensive joining instructions and the Commissioning Course is no exception, with the list ranging from a full-length, plain, black skirt (handmade by my mother as no sensible shop would stock such a thing) to a can of spray starch.

'You are in Two Platoon so up another flight. Just drop off your kit and get your car moved, then back here for the next detail.' She hands me a pin-on name badge, with my rank and surname on yellow embossed Dymo tape, along with a key ring bearing a single key and a metal number disc embossed with the number 112. Then she quickly switches her hawk-like attention to the person behind me and moves on.

There is hushed activity and movement everywhere as the women on my course are signed in and ticked off the lists on the clipboards. We are all nervous and excited that the day has finally arrived for us to start the long-awaited training course. I look at some of the confident young faces of the new arrivals climbing the stairs and wonder who will last the course and whose image will be blacked out of the mugshot photos that are no doubt pinned on some office wall. I'm determined to march out of this place as an officer and not walk out as a civilian who has failed to make the grade.

I've barely spoken a word to any other cadet yet. We make eye contact as we pass each other in the narrow corridors and perhaps exchange a snatched whisper about which room is which but no one says much – we all seem to know this is not the time. Right now, we are quickly dumping our ironing boards and bags on the floor – no time to unpack – or rushing outside to move our cars or say a hurried goodbye to those parents who have dropped their daughters off. Then it's quickly back to the College.

Once signed in and luggage-free we stand silent in organised rows, a squad of over forty women aged between eighteen and twenty-five, all wearing either a smart skirt or a day dress as per the joining instructions. I'm standing to the right of a tall woman in her early twenties with short dark hair. She looks relaxed and comfortable in her surroundings, unlike some of the wide-eyed youngsters, who are clearly very nervous. Opposite us stands a mute squad of similarly smartly suited and booted male cadets, our mirror company of graduates, who also start today. Male staff circle them like sharks, armed with the now familiar clipboards.

Each company is then marched around the main roads of the Academy, stopping at each building to be told what it is and whether cadets are allowed in it. As we stop outside the swimming pool the tall, dark-haired woman beside me whispers in a distinctly Geordie accent: 'The chlorine is so bloody strong you can barely see a thing all day after swimming in that.'

A woman with long blonde curly hair standing directly

in front of me turns her head a fraction to hiss back: 'How often do we go swimming?' Her gentle Welsh voice sounds worried.

'Not sure, but we definitely have to do the military swimming test . . . wearing uniform.'

'Oh God,' says the Welsh voice, before we move off to the next building.

Under the cover of the clip-clop of heels on tarmac, I learn that the tall Geordie is Moira, who has been here before with the TA, and the Welsh woman with the long curly hair (I can only see the back of her head) is Jane. We stride onwards.

As we come to a stop, an extremely scary sergeant major launches out of one of the buildings to tell us something vitally important:

'Only squirrels and the Commandant*,' he pronounces it 'squirrills', 'are allowed on this grass and as I know you are not the Commandant you must be a squirrill. Squirrills are vermin; vermin should be shot so you might not want to tread on this grass. Ever.'

I still think twice and look both ways before stepping onto mown grass.

In 1989, unlike today's mixed groupings, the male and female cadets at Sandhurst lived and trained in separate companies and platoons. Male companies at Sandhurst have the names of famous battles or campaigns: Blenheim, Salerno, Rhine, Normandy, Waterloo, Marne, Burma and Amiens. We are Edinburgh Company, which strikes me

---

* A commandant is the head of a training establishment.

as wimpy in comparison – it sounds more like a hen night
location or a company that makes woollen goods rather
than an overseas historic battle honour. There are two in-
takes a year, in January and September, so the only other
female company is Windsor Company, which is made
up of those cadets who started in September, just a few
months before us. My course is WSC (Women's Standard
Course) 891, January intake of 1989. Graduates and all
female cadets complete an eight-month, two-term course
in ugly Victory College, while male non-graduates endure
a full-year stint in the Academy's magnificent New College and stately Old College. We share the dining room
and bar (closed for the first five weeks) with our male
graduate cadet counterparts but we sit at separate tables as
fraternising is strictly forbidden for now.

'Don't look at him Miss Stephens, he's got nothing you
need,' shouts Staff Beech when she catches me making eye
contact with a male cadet across a crowded dining room.

As I quickly learn, everything in the Army is organised
to the nth degree and is mostly done alphabetically using
surnames, so as my name is 'Stephens' my monastically tiny
room, with its wincingly garish bright orange paintwork
and drab blue curtains, is between Jane Souch, the Welsh
curly haired woman in front of me during the walkabout,
and Moira Watson, the tall Geordie who's been here
before. Opposite is Cath Pearson, who already seems to
know everyone (although I'm not sure how), and Claire
'Pridge' Pridgeon, who seems to know nothing. All cadets
bar one are younger than me and the youngest, Bernie, is
not quite eighteen so she is immediately christened 'Baby
Bernie'. There is a real mix of women, from giggly girls to

serious bluestockings, but only Jane is married. Some have
come from Army families, so are comfortable in familiar
surroundings, while others like Pridge have no military
experience at all so must be finding their new home very
alien.

All of the rooms have the same basic equipment and
layout: an orange cabin-style bed with drawers underneath
for equipment and uniform; a small orange wardrobe
beside the orange sink unit; a grey desk with three orange
shelves above; one wooden desk chair and one drab soft
armchair, or 'Chair, Easy, Low-Back', which is its official
title.* There is a plastic laundry bin with a hinged lid that is
strong enough to sit on and a metal wastepaper bin. Only
the two chairs and the two bins can be moved as all the
other features are firmly built in. With nothing allowed
on the walls and just a small cork noticeboard above the
desk (everything on the noticeboard must have a drawing
pin at each corner like the one in the entrance lodge) there
is little opportunity for any personalisation or variation
at all.

This first day at Sandhurst is a whirlwind of activity,
all governed by precise rules and procedures. We are each
handed a red tracksuit by a staff sergeant – we won't be
wearing civilian clothes at all for the next five weeks – and
are given a few minutes to change into it and unpack our
luggage, leaving the empty cases in the luggage room at the
end of the corridor. Pridge is clearly destined to be the platoon comedian as we laugh at her disgust of the horrendous

---

* All MoD furniture has an official title for ease of ticking off on clipboards.
I have spent many hours stock-checking furniture.

plasticky red tracksuit. 'I look like a bloody garden

gnome,' she wails, posing with an imaginary fishing rod. Just as she strikes her pose, there's a groan from one of the cadets in a room down the corridor as she discovers a porn magazine in the drawers under her bed.

Cases emptied, it's off downstairs to the dining room for some Olympic-level form filling. There is so much documentation, from making a will to signing the Official Secrets Act, which will apply for the rest of our lives. An admin sergeant guides us through the piles of triplicate paperwork on the rows of tables laid out in the functional school-style dining room.

While queuing for my turn at a table I learn that your next of kin is legally your father, so his is the only name allowed on the emergency contact form. One cadet is horrified.

'I haven't seen my father since I was two so can I put my mother down?' The admin sergeant shakes his head. No, she can't. They will track down her father and ask him to contact her mother if anything unfortunate happens. Nice.

At a neighbouring table, a red-haired, green-eyed cadet is asked what colour her eyes are for the ID form.

'Green,' she replies.

'Blue or brown?' asks the admin sergeant.

'They're green,' the cadet insists.

The sergeant sighs deeply. 'Blue. Or. Brown?' he says.

'Neither actually. As you can see, they are very green, emerald green really.'

Another sigh. 'BLUE . . . OR . . . BROWN?'

'Um, blue?' comes the tentative response.

'Now you're learning.'

There is a similar issue with relationships; once married, your spouse becomes your next of kin and is to be informed immediately and considerately if anything should happen to you, but right up until your wedding day they are your 'friend' and appear at the very bottom of the contact list below 'Other nominees', to be informed by one means or another when someone gets round to it.

Once we have filled in the last page, on which we list the sports in which we pretend we are competent, we file out of the hall and go upstairs to our platoon classrooms in a neighbouring wing of the building. We sit silently in rows of school-type desks according to the regulation seating plan; that is, in alphabetical order. As an 'S' I am on the aisle in the back row, which means I have to squint to see the blackboard. A clear authoritative female voice outside the door commands: 'Two Platoon, stand!'

The silence is broken by a cacophony of scraping chairs as we stand up straight and watch a short, blonde-bobbed female captain in her late twenties walk down the centre of the room to the front of the class, followed by her yellow Labrador, who stops at my desk and flumps down beside me.

'Do sit down ladies,' says the trim captain.

As we dutifully sit, one of the staff sergeants from our welcoming committee strides purposefully down the aisle to join the captain at the front.

'My name is Captain Wallis. I am your platoon commander and this is Staff Sergeant Beech, who is Two Platoon's staff sergeant. During your first five weeks here,

Staff Beech will be the main focus of your daily routine and I will be instructing you for some of your lessons.'

We all look at Staff Beech, also in her late twenties, with renewed interest, taking in the steely glint in her eye that is only slightly diminished by her red lipstick and the glossy brown curls scraped into a neat bun at the nape of her neck. Her clear authoritative voice echoes round the hall as she says: 'I'll be settling you in, guiding you through the first five weeks and showing you how to present and care for your kit as well as teaching you drill. You come to me if you have any problems or issues.' I quickly decide that I don't have any problems or issues.

The initial welcome is about getting us processed quickly and is a sudden plunge into the cold bath that is military life. The officers will be present but at a distance, so we know they are there, but they will let the staff sergeants and the Company Sergeant Major do their job of sorting us out for the first critical five weeks, when we are learning to be soldiers. Later, the officers come to the fore and the staff sergeants drop more into the background.

Captain Wallis explains the basic organisation of our female company: one lieutenant colonel, three captains, one company sergeant major, two staff sergeants (one of which is Beech) and an admin corporal. All competent, highly experienced women whose job it is to weed out the weak performers and mould the rest of us into officers over the next eight months.

We are asked to introduce ourselves by surname and previous occupation, so I discover that Cath and Jane are both qualified teachers who are joining the Educational Corps and have already met each other during the lengthy selection process. Jane is the first married woman to be a cadet at Sandhurst so she is addressed as 'Mrs' to everyone else's 'Miss', something the instructors struggle with daily. Also, as a Welsh national hockey player, she is fitter than me by far. Cath appears very serious on the surface but has a dry wit that has us in stitches – usually just at the wrong moment. Moira, a tall Geordie, is a Hadrian's Wall archaeologist, which the staff say will come in handy when it comes to digging trenches. She doesn't look pleased. As a veteran of the University Officer Training Corps[*] she went on to become an officer in the Territorial Army, so she has been to Sandhurst before, although only for a couple of weeks. I quickly come to rely on her military wisdom to help me keep up and she is very patient with me. Claire 'Pridge' Pridgeon is desperately keen to excel at everything military, despite having only worked in an office before, and has the least experience of all of us.

The few of us at the end of the alphabet, and therefore at the end of the corridor, quickly become firm friends, helping each other through every aspect of this strange military life. It seems such a lottery that our closest friends will be determined by the first letter of their surnames. Little did Cath and I know that thirty years later our sons would go to university together, one a historian and one a physicist. It's a small world.

While we wait patiently in yet another queue in the stores, this time being issued with our flat black lace-up

---

[*] A non-combatant unit attached to universities. Many graduate cadets have experienced military training via this route.

shoes,* Cath, Moira, Pridge and I look carefully at the
pin-on name badges that we've each transferred onto
the revolting red tracksuits. Mine reads 'OCdt Stephens',
officer cadet I surmise, the same as Pridge. Cath's badge
reads '2Lt Pearson', showing that as a university graduate
she will start one rank higher (second lieutenant) to give
her an enhanced salary. I glance around at Jane's and the
other women's name badges – Pridge and I seem to be in
the minority as most of the company are graduates. Some
of the other non-graduate women have served as soldiers
for years and have been spotted for their potential and
picked for Sandhurst.

'You lot will be quids in, since we can't actually spend
anything except on bloody boot-polish and spray starch
for the first five weeks,' I say, suddenly very aware of the
fact that I have taken an almost 50 per cent pay cut to do
this.

'It doesn't quite work like that. They keep our extra
pay until the end of the course so we all get the same
daily rate while we're here, like,' says Moira, slipping in a
bit of Geordie for a joke. 'It's a nice little bonus but that's
months away. We're really only second lieutenants on
paper. They call us Mr and Miss but soldiers don't salute
us, not until after midnight on Commissioning Day, when
we turn into proper officers.'

That dream, to become an officer, was clearly one that
I shared with all the women around me and it begins to
dawn on me just how many obstacles we are about to face
while being heavily outnumbered in this male-dominated

---

* Civilian size 5½ turns out to be an Army size 245L – who knew?

world.

Along with our ranks we have to work out abbreviations for ourselves, but out of the million or so acronyms and abbreviations that the Army loves so much we are issued a list of the basic ones and are expected to learn them like a French vocabulary test at school.*

'What the bloody hell is a BFT?' asks Jane of no one in particular as she calls out from her room, her voice revealing her exasperation. 'We have to do a practice one, whatever it is, next Friday according to this timetable,' she continues. She steps out of her room into the corridor so we can hear her, waving a folded sheet of paper that tells us what is happening when and where and while wearing which outfit in our first few weeks. This is the most important of the sheaves of paper issued on the first day. Jane is alone in the empty corridor and the hiss of steam irons is the only sound emanating from the surrounding rooms. One cadet is now deeply regretting bringing a tiny travel iron. Directed and overseen by the omnipresent Staff Beech, the marathon task of ironing the creases out of and then into all the newly issued clothing is under way. As well as uniforms and a stripy bedcover, we have just collected stacks of sheets and blankets from the stores

---

* I've gone on to collect acronyms and abbreviations throughout my career. A renowned one belonged to a neighbour who had the pleasure of being the Military Assistant to the Director General of Individual Training and this meant that his post was officially called MADGIT, which looked wonderful under his signature on letters. My personal favourite refers to the layout of an Armoured Brigade Headquarters on operations, where armoured command vehicles reverse into a circle and the space between them is covered in canvas. It's called an FBT formation – Fucking Big Tent. Most things in the Army seem to have an 'F' in them somewhere.

and are working our way through them. After we've ironed them we put them into the wardrobe and drawers according to the very detailed guide that Staff Beech handed out.

'The BFT would be the Basic Fitness Test,' calls Moira, the fount of all military knowledge, from her neighbouring room.

'And what on earth is that?' asks Jane.

'It's all the fun of a three-mile timed run. You normally have to do it every couple of months or so, but here I think it's monthly if not bloody daily . . .' Moira puts her head round the door to see the expression on Jane's face.

'That doesn't sound too bad,' Jane shrugs. 'I run miles up and down a hockey pitch all the time in training, so I should be OK.'

'Well, you have to run a mile and a half in squad then line up and sprint the last mile and half as fast as you can. You can at least wear trainers, so it's easier than the Combat Fitness Test. That's an eight-mile timed squad march where you run in boots carrying all your kit, helmet and weapon.'

'I've never run in squad before – everyone's so bloody close together, don't you keep bumping into the person in front of you?' Jane asks in her soft, distinctive Welsh accent.

Personally, I'm more worried about the mountain of precision ironing that's got to be done within the next thirty minutes than a run next week.

'No, running in squad is really easy, much easier than running on your own. You just get in step with the person

27

in front and switch off completely – the time just flies by. Focus on the movement of their shoulders or their hair and it's quite hypnotic,' Moira smiles. 'Anyway, how's the ironing going?'

'I've done all the shirts, skirts, trousers and PT knickers so now I'm just ironing the socks,' calls Jane, back at her beloved ironing board.

Cath, Moira and I rapidly appear in Jane's doorway – this we have to see. 'You're ironing fucking socks?' we say in unison. Jane looks up and shrugs, as if it's the most normal thing in the world.

Once we've finished ironing, we move on to hours of polishing shoes and boots, again under the ever-watchful scrutiny of Staff Beech, who patrols the corridors silently, looming behind me when I least expect her. We sit on the floor of the stone corridor outside our rooms so there's no chance of any stray polish finding its way onto the precious carpet tiles. Cath and I are perched on our upturned waste bins which double as a stool, each with a shoe wedged onto our left hands, while Pridge and Moira sit cross-legged surrounded by tins of polish, cloths and pots of water. There are just twelve of us from Two Platoon downstairs, with the rest of the company on the floor above us, so it's much quieter down here.

After balancing a glistening flat black lace-up shoe on my knee I dip a finger wrapped with soft cloth into a pot of water and then into a tin of black Parade Gloss shoe polish. Finally, I press down on the leather toecap, moving my finger in small, tight circles. It's often said that your shoes spend more time on your hands than on your feet at Sandhurst. I learned intense polishing or bulling in my initial TA training, so I'm also trying to memorise all the sheets of information laid on the floor beside me as I polish.

During the day, it had become increasingly clear to me that I am distinctly less knowledgeable about military life than most of the women in my company. However, luckily for me, Moira has considerable knowledge of military matters, so I always have someone to pester with all my silly questions. It's the little things that give away military experience; due to my stint at the TA, I already knew never to lean against a wall or to put my hands in my pockets. Poor Pridge, however, has come straight from a totally civilian life, working in the City, and has absolutely no knowledge of anything military except what she's been able to read during the selection process, so from day one we all try to help her out until she can catch up. Something I learn during my time at Sandhurst is that there is always someone worse off than you and if my learning curve is steep then Pridge has a vertical one.

My somewhat less than extensive knowledge of Army ranks is based on watching *Dad's Army* on TV as a child in the 1970s, so I understand the relationship between Private Pike, Corporal Jones, Sergeant Wilson and Captain Mainwaring, but I don't know much more about ranks other than the basic tiers. I've realised that the most important abbreviation in my life at the moment seems to be NCO or non-commissioned officer, which means any soldier above the rank of private and below a sergeant major. After studying the top sheet diligently, I declare: 'I think I've got this now, see if I'm right so far – the bottom soldier rank starts at private . . .'

'Wrong!' shout at least three voices from down the corridor.

'Sometimes it's gunner,' says Moira, having served in TA Artillery, 'or driver.'

'Guardsman or trooper,' calls Ali.

'Sapper or signaller,' shouts Tana.

'Oh God!'

It turns out, according to my Service Writing textbook, that there is also kingsman, airtrooper, fusilier, craftsman, ranger, rifleman or musician. Even staff sergeants are sometimes titled colour sergeants depending on which bit of the Army they are from, so it takes a while to get my head around the myriad of soldier ranks, but at least the officers are easier to understand.

Although we are all soldiers in the broadest sense there are two very distinct career streams in the Army – one for officers and one for soldiers. I want to be an officer so, coming straight from the civilian world, I must first pass the Commissioning Course at Sandhurst. This is the same for both the part-time Territorial and the full-time Regular Army. The lowest rank on the officer career tree is officer cadet – a real no-man's land, as cadets are neither proper officers nor soldiers.

'So let me get this right,' I say, '. . . as a non-grad, I am currently an officer cadet and then will be a second lieutenant* for exactly two years after Sandhurst regardless of what job I do or how well or badly I do it?' This seems unfair somehow. 'And I'm automatically promoted to

---

* Pronounced lef-tenant in the Army but letenant in the Royal Navy. Don't ask.

lieutenant after two years?'

'Yep – you should've gone to uni!' jokes Moira. 'Don't forget that we grads only get one pip instead of two in our first year, even though we're actually full lieutenants. We'll be "one-pip wonders".* It's a bit like wearing L plates. They don't want anybody thinking that we know what we're doing!'

Not for the first time, I appreciate that it must be very hard for someone of Moira's experience to start again at the bottom rung of the ladder.

'If you pass the practical tactics exam you'll be a captain after a few years, but that's the furthest any of us will get on our short-term three-year contracts. If you're fool enough to sign up to become a career officer, though, and survive the Junior Division course at Staff College you can get to be a major and beyond. Mind you, as the WRAC is a corps, the highest a woman can go is brigadier.† It's a shame that I could join the artillery with the TA but not with the Regular Army, otherwise I could be a general!' laughs Moira.

Only men are allowed to join the 'teeth arms' – infantry, armour, artillery,‡ those parts of the Army that directly engage with the enemy – and it is from those teeth arms that the highest ranks of generals are drawn, so women are limited in their progress up the ranks. It's not so much a

---

* New officers wear a single lonely pip (embroidered or metal star insignia) on their shoulder epaulettes.

† Regardless of gender, the head of most supporting groups or corps is a brigadier – a one-star general level.

‡ The Royal Corps of Signals is also considered a teeth arm due to its role in electronic warfare.

glass ceiling as a steel reinforced one. A feeling of frustration at the restrictions on women's employment bubbles inside me, particularly when it means that we can't be promoted beyond a certain point.

Right now, though, I focus back on polishing my shoes as I'm striving just to stay an officer cadet and not be relegated to being a civilian.

2

Spit and Polish

The mounting tension in the speeding Land Rover is suddenly broken by a loud intermittent buzzing. I look quizzically at Corporal Gregg and raise an eyebrow. Now what? Without taking his eyes off the road he nods towards the gap between our seats. The car phone is ringing. I look at it in surprise; I've never used a car phone before. The orange light on the massive brick-like Motorola handset is flashing. I pick it up gingerly.

'Err, hello?' I don't know quite what else I'm supposed to say. This phone number is highly classified so whoever is calling knows exactly who will answer.

'Ops Room here, Ma'am,' a calm male voice replies. 'Just to give you some more info on your call-out, a bloke doing some Sunday afternoon digging in his garden on the new housing estate has dug up what he says is a bomb. The police have taken a look and confirmed that it is some sort of munition. Sounds like a shell but not sure if it's fused – it's less than a foot long and about four inches wide.'

I'm not quite sure how I feel about this new information. At first I'm disappointed that it's not a big iron bomb but I'm also quite relieved that my first call-out is to something less complicated. Although it's not necessarily any less dangerous – you can be killed by a small bomb just the same as with a 1000lb bunker-buster.

'Roger that,' I reply, as I hang up.

'Well, Corporal Gregg, do you want the good news or the bad news?' I ask.

'Definitely the good news,' he says.

'You'll be back home in time for supper.'

'Bugger, that means it's not the Big One then?'

'Not this time. It's probably an artillery shell and we may be able to bring it back with us rather than clear it on site – I'd rather not have to blow it up next to brand-new houses . . . ' I stop in mid-sentence as a thought strikes me – what on earth is an explosive shell doing in the topsoil of a new housing estate? It can only have been a few inches below the surface for a Sunday gardener to find it, so it must have been in the load of earth when it was delivered, probably bought cheaply from one of many decommissioned MoD ranges. In that case the whole estate could be covered in bombs! I reach for the car phone to dial the Duty Field Officer;* this could be a bigger job than I thought . . .

'One minute!' booms the voice in the corridor.

Heart pounding and breathless, I'm tearing off my clothes as fast as I can. I frantically scrabble in the depths of the tiny orange wardrobe for more.

---

* A field officer is a major or above, with a gold braid band on their hat. They are expected to handle any serious issue.

'You should be outside now,' comes the voice again. I fling on a bright yellow Victory College stable belt (a wide webbing belt whose colour denotes a soldier's regiment or corps) and jam a peaked cap down onto my head before launching out of the room like an Exocet missile. Then I bound down the polished stairs two at a time, the metal segs under my glistening black shoes tip-tapping on the stone. Finally, I skid into my position in the squad, close to Glamorous Jo, a stylish and confident eighteen-year-old who always looks as though she has stepped straight from the pages of a glossy magazine – today's no exception. I quickly tuck in my shirt, tighten my belt and straighten my hat before glancing at Moira, who is standing motionless to attention beside me on the other side. Only her heavy breathing reveals that she arrived on the parade square just seconds before me. Jane is next to come flying down the stairs to stand in her allocated spot close to Cath.

At twenty-five I am the second oldest in the company and, while my short experience of the Territorial Army is more than some cadets, I feel woefully inadequate beside some of the bright, fit, capable and confident young women, many fresh from University Officer Training Corps, who are far more accomplished than I. Some, like Glamorous Jo and Baby Bernie, are only eighteen and I know that I could never have done this sort of thing at such a tender age. Three months at sea on *Zebu* gave me confidence and resilience, but I still feel as though I am barely making the grade in some subjects and knowing that my every move is being closely observed by staff looking for a reason to fail me puts me under even greater pressure. Comparing one's performance to others is rarely helpful but I make every effort not to be at the bottom of the pack – it's a competitive business.

Random change parades are a common feature in the early days of Sandhurst training and after only two weeks being here they're quickly becoming my least favourite part of day-to-day life. Staff Beech, our fierce female staff sergeant, calls out a uniform and you have to find it, put it on and stand as a squad, like skittles before the first strike. You are then inspected in minute detail for creases, fluff, lack of polish and any missing items. A twisted shoelace or speck of dust in the welts of your shoes is enough to ruin everything. 'Too much lipstick Miss England,' sighs Staff Beech, as she looks up at Glamorous Jo. She says this daily as more of a greeting than a criticism.

If the entire platoon is perfect, we may only have to repeat the process a few times but if anyone is less than fast and immaculate then we endure this charade through all our umpteen forms of dress and use every piece of carefully ironed clothing. We are then condemned to spend the next few hours ironing everything once again. The precision ironing is compromised when the clothes get creased as you put them on so I have to iron the open necked collar while I'm wearing it. My brown neck stripe, an iron burn, is a distinctive souvenir of basic training.

'Leave yourself alone!' barks the commanding voice of Staff Beech. I freeze – it's like grandmother's footsteps – but as soon as she looks away there is widespread frenzied movement; skirts smoothed and pleats adjusted. Eventually the last cadet ambles nonchalantly into position and is promptly roasted for her lack of urgency, poor attitude and general slovenliness. She has a creased skirt. We curse her silently – this means we will have to do it all over again.

'You have one last chance to get it right. This time it's your Blues, Number One Dress, you have three minutes – Go!'

We sprint away from the parade ground and leap up the stairs like a herd of gazelles, calculating how long it will take to change into the dark midnight blue of the Sandhurst parade uniform, which requires a different colour of tights, and hoping that the shambolic cadet has prepared this outfit for once. You are only as strong as the weakest link is the message that we are painfully grasping, as well as the necessity of having all your kit ready for immediate use at all times. Both are life-saving military lessons.

Being pristine in your appearance, particularly during the initial five weeks, is so important since it hinges on attention to detail – another critical attribute. Those with long hair have the added hassle that it has to be in a neat bun under a hair net using clips painted the same colour as their hair, while short styles like mine and Pridge's must not touch the collar, so we both needed a trim after a few weeks to avoid yet more punishment. Moira had the foresight and prior knowledge to have the back of her hair cut very short at the start. The barber's shop within Sandhurst is only for the male cadets, who can get a quick trim in just a few minutes. We are expected to make appointments at a hairdresser's in town – very time consuming, not to mention unjust, as we are not allowed to leave the Academy anyway. The solution to this conundrum is Glamorous Jo with her trusty scissors, who gives me the necessary trim without breaking the rules.

Strict obedience to the rules is taught by the use of drill

movements, or the complicated co-ordination of one's body to precise positions on command. The art of drill is a major part of the military syllabus and it is practised by armed forces the world over. We soon discover that drill is physically exhausting and very confusing; the more you overthink which arm goes with which leg the harder it becomes. You just have to listen to the instruction and carry out the corresponding movement instantly and without conscious thought; unthinking spontaneous reaction is what drill is all about – blind obedience to a spoken command. In the heat of battle it is vital to have instant obedience to an order, whether it is 'Cease firing' or 'Go left'. Eventually it becomes so automatic that your body reacts with muscle memory and just does what you have been trained to do instinctively.

One morning, as we start our drill lesson on the College parade square, with each platoon forming two lines, we line up in height order with the smallest in the middle and the tallest at either end. Tall, Glamorous Jo and Moira are at either end of one line while two other cadets, Diddy Denys (creatively nicknamed for being quite short) and Rose (small but loud), are in the middle of another. I stand somewhere in between, close to Moira. Since we are supposed to stand motionless, I need to see the end of the line out of the corner of my eye so I can judge where I ought to be in relation to everyone else – it's a complicated business just standing still. Posture must be perfect: shoulders back, chest out, stomach in, hips level, chin up and standing square.

During training I grow an inch in height, simply because I learn to stand up straight. We learn the moves by counting and shouting out numbers – 'Two, Three, Down'

– with each step having a set series of moves. The ritual test of 'passing off the square' means you have mastered all the basic drill moves and passed a major milestone. You can't pass off or march to music if you are wearing trainers, so the slightest injury to your feet or legs means you fall behind in drill lessons as well as PE, or PT, as the forces call the nightmare of getting and keeping physically fit. Occasionally male officers come to watch us, then mutter to our staff before disappearing again. Swinging your arms to shoulder height as you march creates raw chafed patches on the insides of your arms and lace-trimmed bras become cheese graters that saw into tender flesh. Drill after numerous vaccinations (I'm still not sure what disease they thought we would catch) is particular torture, as we fling our arms to shoulder height then press shoulder to shoulder for slow marches.

The first five weeks at Sandhurst are devoted to the basic military syllabus – we're learning how to be soldiers before focusing on training to be officers. It is an inexorable schedule of continual inspections, endless drill, hours of weapons handling, much map reading, relentless rules and ruthless regulations to get us to think like trained soldiers and not the slack, inefficient, disorganised civilians we arrived as. We are so short of time that we often don't have a spare moment to sit down for lunch or even to eat it at all. I scoot into the dining room, grab a plate, accept whatever is heaped on it and eat as much as I physically can while walking directly to the dirty plate area. Then I leave the unfinished meal and run back out again just a minute or two after I ran in.

At this early point in our Sandhurst training, Cath, Jane, Moira and I are trying to keep up with the relentless pace of the eighteen-hour Army day; we are awake and busy cleaning hours before the cold winter's dawn and crawl exhausted to bed what feels like weeks later. Naturally, we don't actually sleep in our beds, or even sit on them for that matter, because we have spent hours delicately ironing each piece of bedding. I have finally managed to position the centre crease of the striped bedcover so it lines up perfectly with the immaculate razor-sharp crease down the centre of the pillowcase. After that, I have absolutely no intention of actually sleeping anywhere near this masterpiece – my bed is a work of art. 'I wish my mother could see this. It would make her nurse's heart sing,' I mutter, as I admire the meticulously folded hospital corners, pristine smooth sheet and untouched pillowcase.

I unroll my soldier's thin grey rollmat, then lie on the floor like everyone else and try to snatch some shuteye. Now that I've been here for over a month I'm so shattered I can sleep anywhere. But I already know that all my efforts will come to nothing as the diminutive yet mightily scary Staff Beech will rip it apart with all the glee and gusto of a four-year-old tearing open Christmas presents. What I don't yet know is which words will be said about my attempt to get it right. As well as acronyms and abbreviations, I'm having to learn this new strange language of Army speak. I quickly discover the words she uses to describe the cleanliness of my room: 'gopping' and 'minging' are not good. 'Not good enough, do it again,' seems to be this week's mantra; the same as last week's, as it happens.

Joining the Armed Forces, in any capacity, involves a

new wardrobe of phenomenal scope. The vast array of outfits, from charcoal-lined chemical protection suits and padded winter liners to blingy dress uniforms, could compete favourably with any fashionista's collection. There is an outfit for every occasion and every temperature. The extensive clothing range is dwarfed by an eclectic assortment of accessories that is mind-boggling in the extreme, with the novice unable to identify what any particular item is, never mind how or even where to wear it. There are strange strappy things that would warm the cockles of a bondage fetishist's heart and there are even elastic ties to ensure the trouser cuffs hang just so. The complex rules governing what goes with what are just as baffling to the uninitiated.

Besides being immaculately dressed, all cadets have to keep their ID, room keys and paper and pencil about their person at all times, but as usual the women's uniforms have no pockets whereas the men's have six. Even male baby clothes have pockets so why does women's clothing always come without them? Do we not need to carry things, or are we supposed to lug a handbag around at all times? Our Sandhurst solution is to put everything inside our hats. We wear quite tall peaked forage caps that are navy blue with a red band and these have a large space above the cap badge with smaller spaces around the sides, so we can even hide a packet of mints as well. The only downside is that a swift 'eyes right' manoeuvre to a passing officer means a loud jangling sound from the squad, as all the keys dislodge from one side of the hat to the other.

Having been issued with the entire contents of a gentleman's outfitters' stockroom combined with Marks and

Spencer's ladies' range circa 1965, we are of course tasked with ironing everything with laser-guided accuracy and storing it in precisely the right place – to the millimetre.

If you think that the ironing is over the top, you should try the cleaning. Here at Sandhurst, clean means shiny – 'see your face in it' shiny or for shoes it is 'see your pants in them' shiny. The last few minutes before any inspection are a whirl of feverish activity as final touches are put to both body and room. Upstairs, Rose is cramming all her possessions into black bin liners to hide them in the luggage room, as this is far easier than cleaning and tidying them. We have all learned a few short cuts to the cat and mouse game of these daily inspections. I have a suitcase containing spare TA uniforms, which are kept in pristine, never-to-be-actually-worn condition just so I can pass muster. I'm not the only one doing this as many others have a secret stash of spare kit that is just for looking at. Most of it doesn't even fit but who cares so long as it gleams? Poor Pridge hasn't served anywhere else so she's only got the Sandhurst-issued kit. As a result, she actually has to wear the stuff that's on show, but her determination to get things right means she often escapes the inspections relatively unscathed.

As the staff sergeants get near our rooms, Cath jams cotton wool up her leaky basin tap at the last minute to prevent a drip spoiling the shiny dry sink. 'I have to time this just right,' she moans. 'If I block it up early it soaks up too much water and falls out just as Staff sodding Beechnut gets to my room.'

Moira and I stand face to face in the corridor (to avoid any debris getting on our carpets) and frantically pat each

other down with Sellotape wrapped around our hands. It's the only way to remove the scourge that is the dreaded 'fluff'. We have carefully used razors to shave the merest hint of a bobble from our jumpers. Jane is the queen of the hoover, with the noise resonating until we hear footsteps above our heads that denote the arrival of the inspecting staff. The click-clack of their metal-tipped shoes acts as the perfect warning signal of their approach. Being downstairs allows us to hear the clang of the metal waste bin being flung to one side overhead and the shouts of disgust, so we are warned about how bad it's likely to be. We stand stiffly to attention outside our doors as the inspecting staff approach. I feel like a mouse under the gaze of a hawk – any flicker of a movement and I'm dead. The Duty Student typically accompanies Staff Beech or, for a more important inspection, Captain Wallis, to religiously record the names and resulting punishment of any failing cadet. It's usually a long list. We polish and bull everything, even the underside of the bin. Woe betide anyone who actually puts anything in either the wastepaper bin or the laundry bin.*
No, these items are purely there to be cleaned and buffed to perfection and are never used for their stated mythical purpose. A bit like the bloody bed then.

After the first five weeks, those few found unsuitable have been weeded out and those struggling have survived closer scrutiny – or not. The transformation from slack civilian to smart soldier is complete in this first phase of training.

---

* The laundry bin is known as a 'dhobi bin', reflecting the influence of the Army's history in India.

Now that we are more comfortable in the military environment our training will develop us to become officers. We will also be able to associate at the College bar and host parties (always fancy dress) with the male cadets of Victory College, Amiens Company. We haven't been allowed to fraternise with them until now. The regime can now relax a fraction. There are no more room inspections or change parades and we are allowed a leisurely lie-in – till 06.30. Bliss!

In our classroom lessons on military law and documentation I continue to sit at the very back squinting to read the board, so Captain Wallis orders me to wear my glasses. I've been reluctant to wear them as that's yet another bloody thing to keep spotlessly clean on inspections. Whenever I am the Platoon Duty Student I have to march the remainder of the platoon around the Academy on the way to our lessons in various buildings, so I need eagle eyes to spot an officer in the distance who needs to be saluted by the entire squad. After a humiliating roasting for failing to salute a uniformed captain (in my defence, he was wearing an unusual red Medical Corps jumper, so how was I supposed to know?), I resort to ordering the platoon to salute anyone in uniform without stripes on their arm, just to be safe. I'm soon soundly castigated by the other cadets. 'Put your bloody goggles on Lucy, we've just saluted the sodding postman!' they shout. I start to wear my glasses.

During our eight months of training some military lessons are taught in the formal classrooms by our female platoon commanders, but specialist subjects have specific instructors; some are middle-aged civilians lecturing on war studies and international affairs while others are ambitious young infantry colour sergeants teaching us skill-at-arms★ and fieldcraft† out on the ranges and training areas. Our popular tactics instructor, Captain Stafford, is a kilt-wearing member of a Scottish regiment who says he was only allocated to teaching the WRAC cadets because he wore a skirt.

One afternoon, after a lecture to both the male and female cadets of Victory College on the realities of war, Captain Stafford opens up about his experience of combat. As a junior infantry officer he deployed to the 1982 Falklands war, only to be shot right at the start of one of the major land battles. His description of the shock of combat and the hours lying injured on the dark battlefield overnight, while his comrades fought all around him, is so vivid and heartfelt that the enormity of our chosen profession really hits home. 'I know that many of you will see operational service in the hot spots around the world over the coming years as women's roles develop within the Army,' he correctly predicts. 'I have every confidence that you will perform as well if not better than your male counterparts.'

After one particular lesson on giving tactical orders to troops we all spend hours diligently making models of the terrain to illustrate our plan, writing and preparing our battlefield analysis for the following day. Captain Stafford is impressed with the thoroughness and care taken in our preparation.

★ Weapon handling and shooting.
† Camouflage, hand signals and sneaking about quietly.

'I know that the vast majority of you female cadets can perform above the level of the average male cadet,' he announces. We trust his opinion, so this comment definitely gives us a much-needed confidence boost. 'You all try much harder and work together so that no one lets the side down – you don't just try to wing it like some of the blokes,' he continues. Part of the rationale for this assumption is that no one questions why a man might want to join the Army whereas, back in 1989, women had to continually justify, explain and defend their decision to join up. So it was never done lightly or because they couldn't think of anything else to do. We are doubly determined to succeed because failure is not an option worth thinking about. We all have something to prove.

Captain Stafford's opinion is confirmed a few months later when Charlie Tipper, a female cadet from One Platoon, becomes the first woman to be awarded the Queen's Medal for achieving the highest scores in military, practical and academic studies. As soon as we hear the news we are all elated as we realise that this sends a clear and timely message to the wider Army that female officers have proved beyond doubt that they can make the grade.

For the majority of our training over the next seven months or so we are paired with Amiens Company, the only male graduate company at Sandhurst at the time, who share Victory College with us. Although we mostly train in our separate platoons and companies, we will be alongside the men for central lectures and demonstrations and for certain subjects we will be mixed with the male cadets.

In 1989, the biggest difference between male and female training is that while the male cadets will spend more time on exercise and on the shooting ranges, gaining range qualifications, we spend extra hours learning military law and administration, which will be our 'trade'. Although we did not yet receive identical training to the men, this was a major advance on previous generations of female officers, who had undergone shorter courses at the WRAC College.

'I wish we could get the range qualifications like the blokes,' moans Pridge, as we head back to College from the ranges, leaving the male cadets to carry on shooting. 'But at least we get to shoot pistols, SMGs* and rifles, while the blokes only fire rifles,' she continues. 'Women have only been at Sandhurst for five years, so Captain Wallis didn't do any of this. She did the "flower arranging course"† with eight other women and got no weapons training at all.'

Unsurprisingly, much time is spent throughout the Army, as well as at Sandhurst, in teaching soldiers how to handle weapons and how to shoot. During one training session, the instructor explains the basics of rifle shooting to us very simply: 'If you are right-handed and right-eyed you hold the weapon in your right hand and aim with your right eye, control your breathing and squeeze the trigger.

---

* Sub-machine guns. We were only armed for our defence so did not initially have assault rifles. Some male soldiers, mainly tank crew, are armed with only pistols as there's no room inside the tank for a long weapon.

† Female cadets originally trained at the WRAC College and were driven to Sandhurst for some lectures. Flower arranging was actually only a single lesson but the name stuck.

If you are left-handed and left-eyed you hold the weapon in your left hand and aim with your left eye, control your breathing and squeeze the trigger.'

I immediately put my hand up. 'Colour Sergeant,* would you mind awfully explaining what I should do as I'm right-handed and left-eyed?'

He thinks for a moment and says: 'You just throw it at 'em Ma'am, 'cos that's the only chuffing way you're going to hit 'em.'

I was fine with the weapons handling despite my stiff right hand, but actually hitting the sodding thing I was supposed to be firing at was a whole new skill which largely eluded me, even with a pistol, which you fire with both eyes open. I was bitterly disappointed, as I'd had visions of me as a crack shot, impressing all with my superior shooting skills; I really, *really* wanted to be good at this vital military skill. Although my Army record says I'm an expert shot it's only because I made a deal with the range testing staff – if they promised to put me down as a pass then I promised not to waste the entire company's allocation of ammunition in a vain attempt to hit the right thing the right number of times. Sooner or later my total lack of either talent or ability with a weapon was going to cause a problem.

Luckily for us, as female cadets have been at Sandhurst for five years we are no longer guinea pigs or novelties, so we don't get the staring and hostility that the first set of female cadets must have received. Nevertheless, we still

---

* Staff sergeants in the infantry are called colour sergeants.

feel like an afterthought hidden away in Victory College. By being co-located with only the graduate men we are kept at arm's length from the majority of male cadets in New and Old College – we are an add-on feature, not an integral part of the male-focused system.

One day, during our first term, we enter a lecture hall for a discussion and debate with members of Rowallan Company (an all-male company who needed extra time to prepare before starting officer training) about women in the Army – the same usual tired and clichéd arguments are trotted out. Ho hum. Women will be injured in training, most will fail as they are not up to it, they will lower standards, lack killer instinct, won't be mentally robust enough, will cry, will create jealousies, will synchronise menstrual cycles and so have 'issues' on operations (men seem obsessed with this), will not bond in teams or will bond too well – the list of objections seems endless.

This seems to be the entrenched attitude of some of the male cadets who are not able to train alongside us in Victory College and so have no understanding of what we are capable of. We explain quite eloquently that women have done the most harrowing of jobs in the NHS for decades, they can manage menstruation (thank you), they have the same emotions but different ways of expressing them so they may cry more readily but they don't smack their best mate in the teeth (fighting is even a specific military offence, because it is so prevalent among male soldiers). Standards are set criteria, so you either meet them and pass or you don't and fail, so there can be no reason why women should be specifically barred from even trying.

Many of the arguments about physical strength and

stamina also apply to men trying to join elite units like the SAS, but there is no suggestion that men shouldn't be allowed to try just because so many fail (men occasionally die in the attempt). We clearly win the debate, which was not hard given that we have faced these clichéd objections so many times before. The men can't defend their argument but are just repeating what they have heard. It is clearly not a subject they have really given any serious thought to. But despite trouncing their hackneyed objections to women serving in the forces, we still come away depressed. It's hard to accept that the male would-be cadets on the ten-week pre-Sandhurst course still cling to the Victorian view of women as delicate damsels. I doubt we changed their minds but hopefully we made them question their outdated assumptions before they start their officer training.

Related to our debate, some of our classroom lessons are specifically about the challenges of leadership when a group of women is involved and tricky situations such as the unspoken hierarchy between women. We could expect to be called upon to referee the spats and niggles of all-female communal living. These 'Practical Problems' lessons cover how to survive as ladies in a man's world, including how to handle jealous wives, hopeful husbands, smitten soldiers, amorous officers and any other little pickle that a young lady is likely to get into when left alone in a regiment with 450 men.

Alongside the lessons on managing in a male world, our officers also pass on some sound advice and arm us with a few wily defences against any 'difficulties' we might encounter. In one of these fractionally more relaxed sessions

Captain Wallis advises us: 'Make sure you snaffle your name card as soon as you sit down to a formal dinner night, partly as a souvenir and partly to prevent any wag purloining it and writing an all-too personal message or night-time invitation, such as "Room 2, 1 a.m. and bring your spurs", and then passing it round the table for the amusement of others at your expense. Many of you will begin your careers as assistant adjutants,' she continues, 'which means you are likely to be responsible for organising the seating plan. This gives you the opportunity to make a duplicate set of name cards. This duplicate set gives you the ability to write your own "bon mots" on the joker's name card and send it round the table until it reaches either the Adjutant or the Colonel, when he will be quickly dealt with.'*

How we are referred to gives us a good indication of the attitude of the male officers. Being called a 'Doris' is shorthand for an empty-headed woman but other terms are worse. 'Crack troops' for one. While we attend Sandhurst we are all still members of the Women's Royal Army Corps and any officer who repeatedly pronounces WRAC as 'rack' instead of W-R-A-C can expect some payback. It is viewed as a deliberate attempt to show women in a negative light, because it is pointed out that: 'A rack is something you screw against a wall.' If the slight is not deliberate, then ignorance of how to pronounce the name of the corps is an indication of how low we feature in terms of respect.

---

* The Adjutant is the primary staff officer to the Commanding Officer, the senior captain in a regiment. Very important person.

As Captain Wallis says: 'Never forget that the WRAC are known as "Lionesses" and our capbadge* has a lioness at its heart. Occasionally you will need to be prepared to show that you have claws and teeth to defend yourself.'

We are warned by Captain Wallis to be careful around alcohol, particularly at dinner nights when we will be invited to start with gin and tonics, then move on to red wine and white wine with the meal, then port, Madeira and finally liqueurs, while still being expected to perform well in the cross-country run at six the next morning. Captain Wallis suggests that we: 'Try to devise a party trick, preferably one that involves drinking water, to counteract the alcohol and reduce the chance of drinking too much.' She points out that alcohol could ruin our reputations just as much as our bodies, which would not be able to tolerate as much as the men around us could. Matching the boys drink for drink will do no one any good.

My particular party trick is to drink a pint of water through my nose while humming the National Anthem. I think it's impossible but that gives me the excuse to 'have another go at it' at various points in the evening. It allows me to rehydrate with a few pints of water and miss a couple of rounds of alcohol while my male colleagues hit the booze. Years later, as I am slowly recovering from a lively dinner night, a friend tells me her secret for avoiding alcohol: 'I always drink Pernod and blackcurrant after dinner.'

---

* Literally the badge worn on an Army headdress but it is shorthand for the element of the Army you belong to. I was originally 'capbadged' WRAC but later 'capbadged' Royal Military Police. I was never 'capbadged' Royal Engineers, as they did not accept women at the time.

'Yeugh!' I say. 'A distinctive drink if ever there was one.'

'Exactly, it stinks so much that everyone else is disgusted, so I dare them all to try a taste,' she explains. 'That empties the first glass so I go back to the bar for a refill, only this time it's just pure Ribena in the smelly glass and I can then drink Ribena the rest of the night from a specially marked "pre-mixed" Pernod bottle behind the bar. So long as I dab Pernod behind my ears from my hip-flask every time I go to the loo, I can pretend to be drinking alongside the blokes yet not actually consuming any alcohol at all. I always win the cross-country the next morning as the boys are all trashed.' Genius!

Throughout this second part of our training at Sandhurst, guidance of this sort from more experienced women is a real lifeline to us as young officers and I continue to receive wise counsel from more senior women who let me into their slipstream during my career. One day, shortly after leaving Sandhurst, I am given some sound, never-forgotten advice by a stout lady of a certain age who I'll call Colonel Knight. She is talking to a group of WRAC junior officers about parties and regimental dinners and I'm not really paying attention, as the partying side of Army life is the easy part as far as I can see.

She recalls: 'To be a social success as a woman, in any walk of life, not just the Army, one only needs to get two things right – what to wear and when to leave. What happens in between will look after itself, but you need to get those key elements right. In the Army,' she explains, 'reputations are very important and ladies at dinner nights must think very carefully about their attire so as to give the correct impression. Although all military invitations specify a strict dress code it is the small details that are so important. Your accessories will be key to a successful evening. The one item you must always avoid are tights. Tights are totally unacceptable and must *never* be worn. Don't bother with those horrible holdups either, they are not much better. You *must* wear proper stockings. I, for example, when going to a mess dinner, wear stockings with a suspender belt and a garter and a minimum of six pairs of knickers.' I look up in surprise and begin to pay attention.

'The first pair,' she says, 'are my normal pair from Marks & Spencer's, like everybody else's, and their sole duty is to stay on. On top of these I wear a black leather thong, a leopard skin pair with a zip up the front, then a pair of PE knickers complete with a hanky sewn into the pocket, followed by a see-through crotchless pair and all topped off with some spotty pantomime bloomers.'

You could have heard a pin drop in the room as we stare at her in disbelief. We reckon that's quite 'rock and roll' for an old biddy; we're all rather impressed with Colonel Knight.

She elaborates: 'As the only woman in the regiment you can expect to be sitting on the top table between the Colonel and the guest of honour – usually some ancient general – while your junior friends are at the far ends of the U-shaped table. You will be required to make polite, genteel conversation while everyone else has fun down at the far end; that is, until the port comes out and the games begin. Now, the games are very important as they will demonstrate your character to the rest of the regiment.

The Army is not impressed with pieces of paper or where you went to school; it is your character that is important and the games will reveal your disposition to all present.'

She goes on to explain how the games work: the first game usually involves the two most junior officers, who are seated at each end of the U-shaped table. They have to swap places without being seen. The winner is the first man sitting on the other man's chair. As no one at an Army dinner is ever allowed to leave their place until long after the port, the only way they can swap places unseen is to duck under the table and crawl all the way round, popping up at the other end. To make it a bit of a challenge, everyone kicks them as they pass by under the table and since they are all wearing spurs it is quite a trial. To prove that they went the hard route they each have to steal an item of clothing from someone on the top table: 'Usually they each steal one of the Colonel's spurs but now that you are there, only your warm knickers are a suitable prize to test a young man's mettle.'

Now in full flow, Colonel Knight adds: 'You'll know when the two young officers have been told what they have to do – they'll turn very pale and stop eating altogether! Everyone knows that the winner of the game is the first man to get to the opposite chair wearing your warm knickers on his head. Can you imagine the stress those two young men are under,' she continues, 'crawling around being kicked with spurs while trying to work out how to explain to their parents that they were drummed out of the Army for indecent assault on their very first dinner night? Can you then imagine their relief when they turn the corner towards the top table and see that you are ready with a pair of knickers balanced on each foot, ready for them to take as they go past?' She smiles and looks around her. 'Those two young men will sing your praises for evermore and they will never have a bad word said about you. To them you are a goddess who has saved them from this nightmare!'

Colonel Knight explains that we will be watched carefully so we should keep a straight face and talk to the general – he won't reply because he will be out of breath as he's kicking. 'You must be seen to be joining in while maintaining your dignity, so as soon as the two young men reach the opposite chairs everyone will see on their heads the pantomime bloomers and the see-through crotchless pair and they'll know you're game for a laugh. Your reputation will soar without you having to do any more. You must be prepared to play their games but always on your own terms. If you made the mistake of wearing tights you're scuppered after the first game, but dressed correctly I can produce an item of warm underwear for nine rounds before things turn draughty!'

She advises us to leave the table with one pair of knickers at mid-thigh level, held in place by the garter, so that when, at the bar, some boorish arse starts yet another anti-female story she can stop him in his tracks by pinging the garter and bringing her knees together to allow the knickers to slide down gracefully and pool neatly around her feet. She can then look down in surprise, step out of them and exclaim loudly but contemptuously: 'I don't know about you lot, but he's bored the pants off me already!'

Then to conclude, she counsels: 'You need to show that you can stand up for yourself but take care; you want to stop the inappropriate behaviour without making a new enemy, so be careful not to humiliate unless you really have to.'

Wise words indeed.

Joining the Army is akin to stepping onto another planet. Everything you think you knew or understood is no longer valid and sometimes it is intensely lonely. Time seems to stand still as a whole new world of busy activities and organised purpose opens up before you, but it's hard. As Cath says as we queue, exhausted yet again, for dinner in the College hall: 'A good day at Sandhurst is doing well enough to be able to stay another day.'

There is no time to enjoy the stunning location, revel in the history or worry about the challenges ahead. You've just got to focus on getting through today. After a while we care about nothing beyond the next task. I am desperate to stay and I never seriously consider quitting of my own accord; this is what I want to do. Hadn't I already been through so much to get here? I had burnt all my bridges by resigning my job and letting out my house. I have a mortgage to pay so I have no choice but to stick it out, however bad it gets, and hope the Army doesn't give up on me. I am allowed to keep my car on camp – I'm simply not able to drive it as we are all confined to barracks for the first five weeks. But just the thought of it being there as an emergency escape route helps get me through the toughest bits. It needs to have the engine turned over periodically, so I sit in it with the engine running on Sunday afternoons and imagine myself escaping through the main gate, free from all this stress, never to return. Then I sigh, turn the key and limp back to face the next challenge.

We're just starting week six and I am suffering from a minor injury to my Achilles tendon. The swollen tissue rubs against the hard seam of my boots and so becomes more inflamed and more swollen. Without rest or access to icepacks the damage increases each day and could risk everything. We've already lost a few cadets during the first month due to injuries or resignations and I don't want to be 'back-termed', or sent home to recover and then have to join the next intake later in the year. I joined alongside these women and I am determined to be commissioned alongside them too.

In the evenings Staff Beech joins us as we sit in the corridors bulling boots and shoes. She gives us tasks such as standing to talk for a minute on the subject of a Coke can, which allows us to practise the art of speaking with an air of authority, or 'cuff and bluff' – you quickly write notes under your cuff and bluff it out. We realise that you can get away with a wobbly plan so long as you speak sincerely with a high degree of apparent confidence. Men, we now appreciate, have been using this trick for years. My ability to talk in public grows quickly, even when I'm put on the spot and don't have an immediate correct answer. By the end of Sandhurst I can usually come up with something sensible to say even if I don't fully understand the question – a vital skill for later life.

The feeling that we are being set up to fail, however, is one that all female cadets unfortunately experience together. The hardware at Sandhurst, such as the steeple-chase and obstacle courses, is all designed for men so short telegraph poles that are meant to be used as stepping stones for a confident male stride become a completely different, and far harder, obstacle for us. Even the weapons represent an additional barrier to overcome. The pistol grip on the standard issue Browning 9mm pistol is designed for a large male hand, so my thumb can't reach the safety catch at all and I can only reach the trigger with the tip of my finger and not the middle bone. A snatched and inaccurate shot is almost inevitable (although it still doesn't explain my appalling shooting). The male infantry instructors are impressed that we all pass our weapons handling speed tests despite having to constantly slide our hands around and adjust our grip to reach the various mechanisms. Only later, while shooting with the bodyguards in Northern Ireland, did I discover that the Army has a whole range of 9mm pistols to suit smaller hands. Pridge went on to lead a Police Firearms Team and as a senior police officer she was still astounded that she passed the Sandhurst tests with such unsuitable weapons.

3

Curtains at Midnight

Easter marks the halfway point in our training: four months down, four to go. Most of my platoon spend a week of the holidays at home, primarily asleep, before joining some of the graduate male cadets and flying to Switzerland on Exercise Snow Cadet – a week's skiing in Verbier. I've only skied on a dry slope before, so I relish the chance to experience the real thing. Moira and Jane join me in the beginners' group with a couple of the male cadets. The days are spent at ski school and the evenings drinking in the chalet bar; it is wonderful to be free of most of the Academy rules.

The Sandhurst love of fancy-dress parties follows us and a 'bin liner party' is planned. The rules are simple: you can only wear a single black bin liner and no other clothing. Moira, Jane and I spend an hour or so fashioning mini dresses from our bin liners while Rose and Diddy Denys manage to create spectacular ball gowns, though we suspect that more than one liner is used. The male cadets fail to read the simple instructions properly and use just one black bin liner between all of them. The College Adjutant, who is among the staff, is not impressed.

Once back at the Academy there is a change of bedrooms as the senior company of female cadets has left, leaving my company, Edinburgh Company, the only women in Victory College. There are still compulsory church parades where we march in our best uniforms to the impressive Academy Chapel for a church service (virtually everything is compulsory at Sandhurst) but Moira and I can spend Sunday afternoons riding the cavalry chargers across the massive Barossa training area to escape the confines of the College.

No sooner have we arrived back at Sandhurst after the Easter break than we pack up and head off to Wales for a week's adventure training, map reading and Unit Expedition Leader course, while the male cadets take their shooting qualifications back at Sandhurst. I am picked out for my map-reading skills and become one of only two cadets to complete the Joint Service Mountain Expedition Leader qualification, which permits me to lead expeditions around the world so long as they are below the permanent snowline. I will later be given the choice of training for either summer or winter expeditions; that is, jungles or the Arctic. The decision to choose jungles is a no-brainer for me; being very cold really hurts my weak right hand and it doesn't work at all at low temperatures. The Arctic training also involves swimming under the ice then stripping naked to run to a distant tent to get dressed again. Not my idea of fun.

While there are quite a few differences on paper between the training we receive as women and the training the men receive, the main difference for us is the unspoken pressure to perform. All cadets are under constant scrutiny at Sandhurst, being watched and judged on every aspect from humanity to dexterity, but women are under a far greater weight of expectation. Our company staff feel this as much as we do and we are all aware that the 'higher ups' are watching closely and judging our staff's ability to get us to the right standard. If we are learning a complicated new drill movement, we will practise at the side of the College which has no overlooking windows. Here Staff Sergeant Beech and our Sergeant Major guide us more gently through the various steps, the softer tone giving away their need for us to get it right before being watched by others. They clearly want us to succeed and we feel they are on our side more than ever. Major hurdles such as 'Passing off the Square'* are far more tense for our staff than for us, as their right to be at Sandhurst is also being tested. Women in general are clearly on a forward trajectory in the Army and they are placed under the microscope here at Sandhurst. Any weakness or mistake will send us all backwards, so the stakes are high and we are all in this together.

One aspect of Sandhurst's training that clearly requires collaboration is the obstacle course, which involves a team effort to get over the high wall. 'I'll give the boost,' says Moira, as we run towards the massive brick wall that is the next challenge.

'I'll boost too,' I say, seizing the chance to get my breath back as we crouch at the base of the high wall facing each other. Cath stands on tiptoe between us, leaning against

---

* Essentially a practical drill exam for the whole platoon. You can't march to music unless you pass.

the smooth wall with her arms stretched out above her. 'Ready!'

Moira and I crouch down, placing one hand on Cath's knee and one hand under her raised heel. We then quickly stand in unison as she is propelled up the face of the twelve-foot wall. Her gloved hands grip the sharp concrete edge of the top stone and Moira and I push hard against the soles of her boots while she hauls herself up. She can then lean over the wall to help the next cadet. Next up is Jane, who joins Cath on the top. With two people leaning over the top of the wall with outstretched arms to catch each member of our team, Moira and I fling them upwards. Once on the wall, each woman twists to face the brick-work then lowers herself down by her fingertips and drops to the ground. When everyone is over, Moira and I take a run up at the wall, planting one foot as high as we can as we leap to reach Cath and Jane's fingertips. There's a frantic scrabble as we lose inches of skin to the razor-sharp top edge but we finally make it onto the wall. As we drop to the ground below the rest of the team are heading for the next obstacle. On we go . . .

While the obstacle course gives us an opportunity to work as a team, the high-level confidence course is very different as it is completed alone. It is essentially an assault course in the treetops close to the College, combining cables, cargo nets, rope swings, scaffolding shuffle bars and narrow gangplanks, all at a dizzying height above the ground. We have run past it on numerous occasions on our way out to the Barossa training area but now we finally have a chance to play on it, to show that we have physical courage or 'bottle' when we are alone. We are wearing combat helmets that are too big for us, like much of the uniform, so they will cause even more injury if anyone falls. The female PT staff remind us to take our time and be careful, as a cadet has been killed falling from this course.

Unusually for a physical training session, the commanders of both platoons, Captain Wallis and Captain Flatley, are here to watch, alongside our company commander, Lieutenant Colonel Wing, a tall, serene-looking woman in her mid-forties with long brown hair in a loose bun. This activity is clearly a big deal if these officers have all come to watch.

We jog on the spot to avoid getting too cold, our breath visibly hanging in the chill damp air around us. The short run over to this area was barely enough to get us breathing hard, never mind warmed up properly. Hands in pockets are absolutely forbidden, so we swing our arms to keep the blood flowing to our bare fingers. As we line up at the first obstacle, I realise that I am relaxed and looking forward to this. This is my forte; if Sandhurst was BBC's *Mastermind* quiz then climbing tall, wobbly things would be my specialist subject. Other cadets around me are quiet and ashen-faced as they try to hide their nerves and fear of heights, but not me. Here I am in my element, so I am keen to make up for what I think is my lacklustre performance in virtually all other areas. I have a good reason to be confident on this test – my *Zebu* experience.

The first obstacle is a tree with large nails sticking out of it as foot and hand holds. We have to climb onto it to reach the cables strung between the trees.

'Come *on* Pridge!' calls Rose.

'Get a move on – it's freezing!' cries Cath.

'How the fuck am I supposed to do this?' responds Pridge.

Pridge is standing on the lowest nail but the course has been built for men so the next nail, meant as an easy foothold, is up near her ear, way out of reach of her foot. What would be a simple ladder-type climb for male cadets now becomes a far harder struggle for those under 5' 6" and Pridge is by no means the shortest cadet. Even the tallest women struggle as they have shorter legs in comparison to most men. After much effort and sheer determination Pridge hauls herself up the tree using arm-power alone and now faces two steel cables between her tree and the next. She must stand on the lower cable and hold the upper one in order to shimmy across the gap. We watch in horror as we realise that the cables, measured with men in mind, are too far apart for us. Pridge hangs from the upper cable with the tips of her toes barely touching the bottom cable and definitely not bearing her weight. In sub-zero temperatures and with bare hands she clings to the steel cable and begins to cross. As she is blessed with immense upper body strength she reaches the second tree. One by one we climb and shimmy . . .

After my months at sea scrambling about in the unstable rigging, I find climbing cargo nets and cables high above the ground much less of a challenge, even though at 5' 6" I can barely reach the next handhold.

When Pridge and Moira have successfully completed the first obstacles the queue shuffles forwards. 'On you go, Miss Stephens,' calls the PT instructor, waving me to the first tree. 'Pause when you reach the second tree to let

Miss Watson get off the wire before you step on.'

One by one we climb the tree and play follow-my-leader through the aerial obstacle course. My confidence increases as I overcome each barrier. I swing on a loose rope and let go at the furthest point of the swing, thrusting one arm out like Superman so that it hooks into the vertical cargo net opposite. Once safely on the net I can climb easily to the top to flip over and work my way down the other side; this feels like old times up in the rigging of *Zebu*. I clear the obstacles one by one with a sense of immense satisfaction. Even balancing on the scaffolding bars to shuffle along them, stand, pause and say my number, rank and name before shuffling to the end holds no terrors. I'm delighted to successfully finish a testing course that so many men will have failed to complete.

Unfortunately, not everyone manages to complete the course with as few problems as Pridge and me. One cadet freezes at the highest point of the aerial course when the pole she is clinging to begins to wobble in the breeze and she can't reach the next one. After much shouting of advice from the ground, the platoon commanders decide that 'someone' has to go up and talk her down, one step at a time. They look around at our group, staring at us expectantly. This is my cue to 'seize the initiative' and show that I'm a team player as well as having physical courage. 'I'll go, Staff,' I volunteer.

As I can shin up the ropes of the confidence course as fast as if I was running up a flight of stairs two at a time I don't wait to be told, but launch forward and hurl myself up the netting, then along the high shuffle bars, until I get to her. When I reach the terrified, trembling cadet I wrap myself around her position and guide her down while stretching across her, one handhold at a time. She is still visibly shaking when we eventually reach the ground and we are horribly late for dinner that day, but I am chuffed to have been able to help and relieved that I have got something right at long last.

We quickly learn that you can't do things on your own; you need others to help you as it is a team effort with no space for precious individuals or divas – you have to work together. Basic military training is a great leveller and there is no stronger, longer lasting bond than the one that is forged with those you train beside.

The Academy shop sells boxes of disposable hand warmers, which are little sachets of iron and activated carbon that burn hot for an hour or so when you open the packet. With these sachets stuffed inside our flat lace-up shoes and white cotton gloves we can fight off the sub-zero cold on parades, where we stand motionless for long periods.

One freezing winter parade practice we have progressed from wearing thick PT knickers to Lycra cycling shorts, desperately trying to keep warm – but it's not enough. I stand gibbering with cold as the men of Amiens Company march into position beside us for the parade.

'They're not even shivering!' marvels Jane.

'That's because they're wearing layers of thermal trousers and thick socks,' hisses Cath enviously through chattering teeth.

'They should try standing here in fifteen denier tights!' says Moira, as we snicker at the thought.

The Adjutant on horseback then takes his position in

the centre of the parade square, directly behind us. We can hear the steady walk of the horse, but instead of coming to a halt with all four legs standing square as usual we hear a shuffle of hooves and an audible sigh from the grey cavalry charger. 'Dear God, no!' says Cath, as the distinctive sound of gallons of cascading equine urine echoes off the façade of the stately Old College behind us.

The cadet at the far end of our line risks a sneaky backwards glance to see who is directly downstream of the foaming torrent heading straight for us. Down the line flashes the name

'Moira'. Her face is a picture. Her cold blue lips purse with anger at the thought of her perfectly bulled parade shoes being forever ruined if they make contact with the frothing acid that is now flowing her way down the slope of the parade square. There just aren't enough hours in the day to bull a second pair of shoes up to parade standard. 'If that touches my shoes, I'm going to throttle the sodding Adjutant,' mutters Moira.

We continue to stand to attention, motionless but for the shivering – there is absolutely nothing we can do to prevent the inevitable happening in the next few seconds. 'Edinburgh Company!' A distant but urgent female voice is heard clearly above the chattering teeth. 'Edinburgh Company will advance, by the left, quick march!' The rushed words of command come from our Company Sergeant Major, who has spotted the crisis from the other side of the square and has bellowed the magic phrase that allows us to march forward away from the acidic stream that threatened to engulf at least one of us. As we move quickly out of the danger zone to wheel around the square and return to a dry spot of tarmac, we see the Academy Sergeant Major berating our rescuer for the breach of parade format as forcefully as only the Academy Sergeant Major can. Our Warrant Officer defended us, despite a negative consequence for herself, and once again we recognise that the female staff want to help us succeed and that we are all in the same team.

In our final term the training moves on from soldiering and focuses more on leadership skills. One aspect that comes to the fore is social skills, such as how to host guests at dinners and lunches. Again, we work in pairs with Amiens Company, so the second cadet can pick up the conversation when the first has dried up, and we practise the etiquette of introducing people to our guest, usually a member of the Academy staff. We learn the art of getting our guest to talk, acting as a supportive listener and only interjecting to encourage the guest to speak more. The non-speaking host is responsible for keeping the drink topped up and making sure the group moves to the table at the right time. At one Sunday curry lunch a male cadet and I get our practice guest too drunk (I was doing all the talking, so I blame the male cadet). As a result, when our guest went home in the afternoon to cut the grass he mowed the toes off his posh green wellies. We are each 'fined' the cost of a wellington boot.

Much emphasis is also placed on 'officer standards': a rather vague concept that seems to be part manners and part honesty in all things. The social rules are there to make people from different backgrounds feel comfortable and know what is expected of them. It's mostly what the 'done' thing is, such as watching others play sport to show your support rather than spending that precious time selfishly getting your kit ready. We are taught to use the same language so that the midday meal is not dinner but lunch and the evening meal stops being tea or supper and instead becomes dinner, which is at 7.30 p.m. for 8 p.m., in contrast to the soldiers' evening meal which is at 5.30 p.m. Our first dinner night is with our company staff so we can learn the basic format. It's the first experience of a formal dinner for many of us, me included.

Once we're seated at the table one of the male instructors shows us an easy guide to formal dining. 'Make an OK sign with both hands (make a circle with your index finger and thumb then straighten the remaining fingers),' he says. 'Now look down at your hands and you see they make the outline of a "b" with the left hand and a "d" with the right. This stands for "bread" and "drink", so it reminds you that yours is the bread on your left and the drink on your right. For cutlery, start with the outside layer and work your way in. Port goes only from right to left, never leaving contact with the table and the Madeira always follows the port.' Simple, I think to myself; you just need to know the rules.

The second dinner is the traditional Father's Dinner Night* part-way through the course, where cadets host their fathers to demonstrate how they've progressed and to cement their support for their chosen career. There's nothing like the fear of disappointing one's father to focus a wavering cadet. The male cadets and their fathers all look

---

* Now updated to 'Parent's Dinner Night'.

as dashing as James Bond in their black-tie dinner suits while we resemble failed nuns in our long-sleeved high-necked white blouses and ankle-length plain black skirts. It's the outfit we must wear to formal dinners if our mess kit is unavailable, but never have I felt so dowdy and out of place – we visibly don't belong. As I take my seat at the dinner table, I vow never to wear it again.

The new term also marks a change in the nature of the training: more shooting and more week-long exercises traipsing around the south of England practising our infantry skills and the classroom sessions are swapped for presentations in large lecture halls alongside our male counterparts. This brings its own challenges as some of the major presentations, such as those concerning operations in Northern Ireland, are attended by the entire Academy. While the graduate male cadets are fairly accepting of our presence, because they are used to studying alongside us and are aware of the similar nature of our training, the same can't be said for the distant non-graduate male cadets in the other colleges, who stare at us as though we are creatures from another planet.

At the end of each presentation there are a few minutes for questions. As we are heavily outnumbered we feel under great pressure (from ourselves and our female officers) to ask a probing and weighty question, so that everyone recognises that we are engaged and inquiring rather than taking a passive role. Just hearing a female voice from among the massed ranks of male cadets announces to all that we exist. Even the Q&A sessions at Sandhurst are competitive, with cadets vying to ask the best question.

Thankfully, one of our top cadets asks a terrific question and there are appreciative nods from the female staff – so we can all breathe a sigh of relief. In the back of our minds we know that if a man asks a stupid question everyone silently will think he's an idiot, whereas if a woman asks the same question there would be audible groans and mutterings from the male cadets: 'Who let the women in?' or 'And that's why my regiment doesn't allow women.' Once again, we're reminded that we have to be twice as good as the men to be considered half as competent. This contributes to tremendous pressure on each and every one of us to perform at our very best or risk letting the side down. If a female cadet makes a public mistake such as saluting without wearing a hat the men mock outwardly and the women groan inwardly, as it makes our personal mountain just a little harder to climb. We are left in no doubt that we will face more of this once we leave the safety of the Academy and serve alongside some of the less enlightened male officers and soldiers.

The PT sessions have also changed in the final term. Originally, the purpose of these sessions was to raise our personal fitness levels with endurance running and swimming, but now they have a more military-focused nature.

'What do we have to do on a log run, Moira?' asks Cath, reading the timetable for the week ahead.

'Run with a log?' suggests Jane, with deadpan humour.

'It's a telegraph pole with a few rope handles on either side,' says Moira. 'It weighs an absolute ton. Only about six people can run with the log, so the rest of us run behind until we are called to take over. You then have to sprint forwards and swap over, while the person on the log drops back for a breather. The sheer weight of it pulls your arm out of its socket even when you're not trying to run with the damn thing. Did I mention that you carry it for four and a half miles?' she adds.

Wonderful, I thought. *Sounds like zero fun.*

The morning of the dreaded log run arrives, cold and crisp, and I'm conscious of my dodgy wrist. I'm certain it will not be happy having to carry even a fraction of the weight of the massive log. Alongside this worry, I'm conscious that I have to pass this test – one of the hardest challenges for me – if I am to fulfil my dream of becoming an officer. The pressure is making my heart beat faster as I march with the rest of the platoon across to the gym. Moira and Pridge are positioned beside the log at the start point outside the gym, with fingers straining to grip the rope loop as it cuts into their flesh.

'Pick up the log!' orders the PT sergeant. There are grunts of effort as the cumbersome log is hoisted off the ground. I try to stay on the right-hand side of the squad running behind, so I can use my good left arm. We run in silence for the first few minutes, listening carefully to the laboured breathing of those struggling under the weight of the log up front. *How heavy is it? How hard will it be? Will I be able to cope?* These are the questions going through my mind as I run along at the back.

'Mrs Souch, take over this rope!' shouts the female PT instructor. It is thankfully not me this time, but I know my turn will come. 'Oh, God,' Jane mutters under her breath as she sprints to the front and takes the toggle rope from Pridge who immediately drops back, her face reddened with the exertion. She rolls her eyes at me as she

74

matches my step at the back. 'That hurt,' her eyes tell me.

'Miss Stephens, take over here!' comes the order. Here goes. I sprint forwards and my heart sinks as I realise the instructor means me to take over from Moira on the left-hand side of the log, so I will be holding the rope with my crooked right arm. With no time to think, I put the loop of rope in my right hand and take the strain as Moira thankfully falls back. My God, the weight of it! I lean away from the log, trying not to be pulled over by it, and then lean forward to help haul the heavy load along the road. I can do nothing now but hang on and run my heart out. After what feels like hours, but can only have been minutes, I am replaced on the log by Rose and I drop back, exhausted, to run behind. Twice more I am called forward to carry the log as we run around the roads of the Academy. We are on the way back to the gym at last and are clearly spent when I am once again summoned to the front.

'Dig deep!' shouts the PT sergeant, to encourage those flagging on the log. 'Pain is merely a bodily sensation and you should enjoy *all* your bodily sensations,' she yells at us. I have barely enough energy to overtake the other runners and move into position alongside the log. As I take the rope yet again, I am forced to think back to all that I have been through to get to this point. Wasn't my seasickness on *Zebu* worse than this? Didn't I promise myself that I'd never complain about anything ever again if I ever made it to solid ground? Enduring these last few minutes of pure agony is nothing compared to the utter misery I have already survived on *Zebu*. If I can cope with the challenge of months at sea I can cope now. I can do this!

★

One morning I wake up groggy and feel worse as the hours go by. I dare not go sick as missed training time risks being taken off the course. By lunchtime I'm definitely unwell with a relapse of malaria. Feeling shaky and dreadful, I struggle down to lunch. I spend ten minutes trying to put a piece of cheese on a biscuit but by the time I succeed I am too confused to know what to do with the biscuit. In a blur, I follow the others to the main parade square for a drill lesson, where I am pushed and pulled around by the rest of the platoon, who are trying to hide my lack of co-ordination and my general confusion. Cath and Moira can't hide me for long and I am eventually screamed at and sent to jail* for being unable to walk in a straight line. By the time I find my way to the guardroom to hand myself in I am collected by a more sympathetic member of staff and guided back to bed for the rest of the day.

My first attack of malaria had come as a surprise, although it shouldn't have. It was a few months before I decided to enrol at Sandhurst. I had recently returned from my trip to Brazil on Operation Raleigh. While I'd religiously taken the daily anti-malarial tablets before setting off, during the trip and for two weeks after coming home (I am a doctor's daughter so I read the leaflet), just as I stopped taking the pills I began to feel tired. I had just started a twelve-hour shift as a security officer at Stansted Airport when I began to feel cold and miserable and then hot and miserable. After struggling like this for a couple

---

* 'Jail' is actually an office inside the guardroom of New College but the order 'Take her to jail!' is an effective deterrent for the rest of the platoon.

of hours I phoned my doctor, who asked me to come to the surgery immediately. An hour later I was in a hospital isolation ward surrounded by people in masks and gloves. The rest of the week was a blur of tests, needles and groggy sleep. An assortment of overly enthusiastic medical students came to interrogate me. 'Had I been at altitude?' they kept asking, hoping I had some very obscure illness only found in the Andes.

'No, just eighty-five feet above sea level – top of the mast,' I repeatedly insisted. I was clearly 'novelty tropical disease of the week', so a learning opportunity not to be missed, and each nasty disease was considered and discounted as I was measured and prodded. Eventually I was diagnosed with bog-standard malaria, caused by throwing up all the anti-malarial tablets and then being bitten by infected mosquitoes. After treatment I was warned I may have relapses but should be OK in the long run. Sandhurst is no place for a relapse but luckily it only lasts for a few hours.

Once we've spent hours each day cracking the drill basics of starting off, marching in straight lines, turning, stopping and saluting on the hoof, we march to a single drum beat and it all starts to get a bit easier. Eventually we will march with a full military band following behind us, playing stirring military music. We cannot fail to add style and swagger while stepping out to such classics as 'The British Grenadiers'. Marching to music feels very natural; the beat helps keep time and everyone remains in step, even on the most complicated moves. For slow marches we press shoulder to shoulder, arms still, trying to ensure that our

little toes touch the ground first as we glide smoothly
across the tarmac to the slow march of the Royal Regiment of Fusiliers: 'Rule Britannia'.

There are many, many practice parades before our
Sovereign's Parade and they all have the same format.
Wearing the dark navy blue parade uniforms of the
Academy, with yellow flashes on our epaulettes to denote
Edinburgh Company, we march in silence from Victory
College across the culvert covering the Wish Stream, a
stream that runs through the Academy, on our way to
join the platoons of male cadets from both New and Old
Colleges. The only sound is the loud tick-tock of the
metal segs in the soles of our gleaming black flat shoes as
our heels strike the tarmac, keeping time as accurately as a
metronome. As we approach New College, Jane, our lead
cadet, marching alone out in front of us, calls 'Edinburgh
Company!' as a warning of the next command, then two
paces later 'Halt!'. Our left heels strike the ground and we
automatically take one pace forward with our right feet;
then we place the left foot down and drive the right foot
firmly into place beside the static left foot at precisely the
same moment, resulting in a single loud crash.

There is no movement anywhere. More commands are
shouted and the band falls in behind us. We are commanded
to march forwards. 'By the left, quick march!' comes the
order as the band strikes up a familiar regimental march
and we feel a flutter of excitement. It is an exhilarating
feeling of both pride and elation when you sense the music
in your bloodstream and bring yourself to your full height
as you strut your stuff across the main parade square in
front of the beautiful Old College, lined with French guns

captured at Waterloo. We take our place among the other companies on parade, which are broadly divided into Senior and Junior Divisions depending on whether we are due to be commissioned in April or August. All are poised to march circuits of the square, turning and wheeling like the guardsmen in London. There is no hiding place on a parade square so any mistakes on our part will be highly visible, adding to the pressure on each of us to get every step absolutely right.

As we aren't allowed to do drill with weapons (yet another unfair compromise we have to make that the male cadets don't) we have a shiny black painted cane to hold at various angles while the men on parade alongside our company swing rifles. The cane isn't added until we have all mastered the basic moves. Admittedly, they didn't seem odd to us at the time as it was a distinct improvement on not carrying anything at all; female soldiers typically march empty-handed. As we were getting ready for the drill, Moira rightly pointed out: 'At least we've got something in our hands. Can you imagine just standing here like lemons while the blokes do rifle drill?' While that would be worse, unfortunately highly polished canes and white cotton gloves do not go together, so occasionally a cane would catapult across the square with its red-faced owner rushing after it while being screeched at by a livid staff sergeant.

The restriction on weapons is lifted near the end of our course and we are issued with rifles, but we don't have enough time to learn all the drill moves so we carry the canes on our commissioning parade: Sovereign's Parade, the impressive ceremony witnessed by our proud families that marks the successful completion of basic officer training.

One month before Sovereign's Parade we travel to Germany for our final exercise – a mammoth set of trials and challenges that will put all our training to the test. Once at Vogelsang, a former Nazi estate complete with German eagles imprinted across the hillsides with coloured trees, we are flown in Chinook helicopters to carry out ambushes in the valleys. Then we are flown back in a series of Lynx helicopters, which is much more exhilarating than riding in the clapped-out buses of Sandhurst. All the infantry tactics that we've practised at home, such as ambushes and weapon siting, seem so real in a foreign country. Over the next couple of weeks we visit different regiments and experience both tanks and artillery manoeuvres. It's hot and exhausting. I even spend a couple of days in hospital after collapsing with heat exhaustion during an ambush, but we all successfully pass the ordeal and are looking forward to finding out about our first postings when we return to Sandhurst for final parade preparation.

The Adjutant's rehearsal for Sovereign's Parade is one of the lighter moments of the year and is a fun time, where we are allowed to muck about. There are many rehearsals, each one being witnessed by an ever-more senior officer, so the Adjutant's rehearsal, the last of the lighter sessions, is attended by the Academy Adjutant. Rhein Company from all-male Old College 'borrow' a giant inflatable octopus used at a lakeside party and drape it across the Old College roof overlooking the parade square, others abseil SAS-style from the roof and another company hire an ice cream van to hand out lollies on the square. Ypres Company sends a note to say they have gone to Ypres for the day then a Chinook helicopter lands and they march out onto the square. My company dress up in a variety of headgear (but with uniform skirts, platoon T-shirts, ties and the usually forbidden sunglasses) so I'm wearing a jockey's skullcap, having been a groom/rider before joining airport security. It is all in such contrast to the seriousness of the earlier months and as I get dressed in my room and then help Moira with her full Arab headdress I let myself take a breath of relief and think about how far I've come.

The highlight of Sovereign's Parade comes near the end, as the senior cadets being commissioned march up the Grand Steps of Old College and the Academy Adjutant's charger (cavalry horse), Delilah, climbs the two flights of stone steps after them. With our backs to the Parade Square and its packed grandstand of spectators, we know exactly when this occurs as we hear the click of hundreds of cameras above the sound of the military band.

Our Commissioning Ball takes place on the night of the Sovereign's Parade, complete with a full fairground and a casino. It is simply the biggest and best ball we will ever go to. Morale is sky high as we get dressed for the evening. We're allowed to bring a guest so I'm sharing my room with Jane, a childhood friend from Somerset. The corridors are noisy with hairdryers and the excited chatter of women getting ready for the evening of a lifetime. I'm wearing my mess dress for the first time so I feel very special. Even though the mess dress for the Women's Royal Army Corps is a hideous 1960s curtain material in 1989, it is the most glamorous outfit I have. The cream-coloured shift dress is flecked with gold and I wear a green silk sash over one shoulder that swings as I walk. In recent years the only nod to change has been a sweetheart neckline rather than a square one, so we feel very outdated already. Moira, Cath, Jane and I practise sashaying down the corridor in our 'curtains', envious of the male cadets who we know will look timelessly dashing in their slim-fitting mess trousers, gold-trimmed jackets and spurs. While we look like poor relations in comparison to the male cadets, I know that my outfit, though dated, is never going to look as good as it does tonight.

Once I've accidentally flushed the loose end of the sash down the loo a few times it never hangs quite the same. I have already pre-ordered the smart green bolero jacket with gold trimmings that is going to be introduced for the WRAC within months, so we will soon look as smart as the men when sitting at a dinner table. As the night draws on, we all gather at the lakeside with our guests to watch the fireworks display on the lake spell out our course number, WSC 891. Then at midnight we uncover our shiny new shoulder pip. We've made it! Although we each had to pass the test – every test – we couldn't have done it alone. We toast each other by the light of the fireworks. The cocoon of Sandhurst has transformed us from grubby civilians to the butterflies of junior officers.

As I stand beside the lake looking up at the colourful explosions, elated with the relief of having finally made it through the trial that is Sandhurst, I reflect that the Academy has taught me how to act like a soldier and think like an officer. I've learned the importance of comprehensive planning and the acceptance that no matter how well I've planned something it will all go to rat-shit the moment the shooting starts. I've learned to believe that I can do this – whatever 'this' is. I've survived the ordeal, learning about my strengths and the limits to my abilities and this gives me the confidence to face whatever challenges lie ahead.

4

'Voluntold' not Volunteered

I press play on the video recorder and lean back to sip my soft drink. I'm giving a talk on bomb disposal to a youth group who meet in the snug of a local pub. Part of the role of press officer for the bomb disposal regiment is to give lectures to schools and youth organisations. The Royal Engineers offer two general interest lectures: 'Map-making for Peace' and 'Bomb Disposal' – no prizes for guessing which one is the more popular. I love to see the expression of shock and awe on people's faces as they watch the footage of an aircraft dropping cluster bombs on a bridge; it's actually a sales video made by the arms company, so they witness a square kilometre of the earth being virtually evaporated to the background sound of rock music and slick American sales patter. As the young faces, eyes wide, are transfixed by the horror of the advertisement I look around the walls of the snug.

Like many old country pubs, it has an array of vintage farm equipment hanging on display. Having been around farms and horses for years, I test myself to see if I can recognise and identify the hardware – there's a plough-share, a mole trap, some hand sheep shears, a horse collar and wait . . . what's that? There, hanging among the horse brasses above the small bar area is a pitted and slightly rusty alloy tube, just over a foot long. It looks very familiar, so I squint at it and spot that one end is a metal ring encircling the top of three flat vanes. Yep – it's a bomb. A 1kg World War II German incendiary bomb to be precise. I silently congratulate myself on identifying it – 'filled with thermite and possibly contains an explosive element to help spread the initial fire and deter anyone from trying to put it out with a shovel full of sand', I mutter to myself.

How on earth did it end up here among the farming implements? I struggle to focus on the rest of the lecture and am keen to ask the landlady a few questions. After convincing her to let me take the bomb away with me, I carefully pack it in the boot of my car wrapped in a blanket. The following morning I go to work carrying the bomb, intending to put it in the UXO bunker for safekeeping and destruction later.

'You come to work to get rid of those bloody things, Lucy. You're not supposed to bring your own!' says the Colonel, as he sees me walking in.

On our return from our final Sandhurst exercise, which takes place in Germany, when it is clear that we have passed all of the required military skills tests and convinced the staff that we deserve to become commissioned officers, we are informed of our first postings. The educators like Jane, Diddy Denys and Cath are all going to complete a Young Officer's Course before going to their first unit, so they know they will be going to Beaconsfield, but for 'mainstream' WRAC cadets like Pridge, Glamorous Jo and me it is a complete lottery.

'It's all right for you lot, you all know where you're going and you'll still be together but I'll be on my tod and God knows where!' I moan to Cath and Jane.

'Well, you're bound to be near someone in our company,' says Cath, trying to cheer me up.

'You'll probably end up at Guildford,' says Jane. 'Some of the other mainstream people will be going there for sure.'

Speculation is rife and I have assumed that, being older than most, I might be a platoon commander in one of the all-female units,* so I can make use of my greater life experience to look after female platoons of clerks and administrators. Or I might even be training WRAC soldier recruits at the WRAC Centre in Guildford. We sit in one of the Sandhurst anterooms, a formal sitting room that we have so far only entered to meet with the tailor (officers' parade uniforms and mess kit are hand-tailored). On this occasion the soft chairs are arranged in a loose semicircle and we fidget with excitement and trepidation. Lieutenant Colonel Wing is in her element as she works her way round the seated anxious cadets.

'Miss Morton? You are going off to Germany, to Hameln as Assistant Adjutant to the Royal Engineers.' Miss Morton smiles broadly. I know she wanted anywhere but the UK so she's relieved. The tense atmosphere relaxes just a fraction. At least someone got the posting they wanted – this could turn out all right.

---

* There were a couple of all-female WRAC administrative support units near large garrisons in the UK and Germany as well as the WRAC Centre in Guildford.

Eventually Colonel Wing looks at me. I hold my breath because the next two years of my life depend entirely on what she says next – will it be Cyprus? Or Guildford with Glamorous Jo? Will it be the gunners or the girls?

'Miss Stephens?' Pause, while she actually *smiles* at me. Scary.

'Do you have a steady hand?'

'Umm, err no,' I reply, slightly perplexed. 'I've had malaria so I'm still a bit shaky at the moment. I've been off sick with it – you did know,' I answer – not really sure where this was going.

'Oh yes,' says Lieutenant Colonel Wing, frowning and looking rather crestfallen, 'I remember now. Well, um, never mind about that, you're going to be a bomb disposal officer with 33 Engineer Regiment (Explosive Ordnance Disposal) in Chatham!'

I just sit there with my mouth open, dumbstruck. No one has ever mentioned that as even a possibility. Lieutenant Colonel Wing must have carried on round the others but I don't hear a thing. A bomb disposal officer! Oh God!

The existing (1989) rules on the deployment of women derived from the government policy that women could not be used in direct combat and the Executive Committee of the Army Board (ECAB) imposed additional limitations: women were not allowed to serve in any post in peace which would be filled by a man in war, nor were they to be employed in units where their presence could 'make military operations more complicated'. This policy remained in place until a new major study called the Crawford Report, which looked into the changing role of women in British society. The ECAB considered this in

July 1989, just weeks before I left Sandhurst on completion of my training. This report moved the goalposts for
all servicewomen and I was to be one of the very first to
be affected by it.

Shortly after dropping her bombshell on me, Lieutenant Colonel Wing tells me that thanks to the Army rule
change, I am to be the first woman to be operational as a
hands-on bomb disposal officer. I am going to be doing this
important and dangerous job – working on live bombs.
Although I have never been in the running for any of the
prizes for the best cadets, this is the greater prize for me
and I am incredibly flattered that I have been chosen for
this challenge. Out of all the postings it is the best one and,
after the initial shock, I am thrilled at the prospect.

It is all a bit of a blur after that. After everyone has found
out their postings I rush to phone my mother as soon as
we are dismissed. 'I'm going to Chatham in Kent,' I tell
her, without even stopping to think that my news will
worry her.

'Oh good!' she exclaims, audibly relieved. 'I am so
pleased. I won't have to worry about you going to Northern Ireland.'

'. . . and I'm . . . going to be a bomb disposal officer!' I
trill, now very excited by the idea.

Absolute silence.

I wasn't going to be the first woman to pass the bomb
disposal course but I would be the first female operator to
be on the Duty Bomb Disposal Officer Roster alongside
the men. Kate Boxell, the previous WRAC Assistant Adjutant at 33 Engineer Regiment, had completed the course

because her role also included being the unit press officer. She therefore needed to explain, with credibility, how the task was done when a large bomb was discovered and had to field the numerous press enquiries that such a high-profile regiment attracts. At the end of her tour she was briefly replaced by an Oxbridge graduate who, after failing the course twice, left to serve elsewhere. This created an urgent vacancy. As an operational unit the regiment is a top priority, so the WRAC command were tasked to find a suitable replacement. According to Captain Wallis, the regiment's Commanding Officer* demanded: 'Never mind the brains, just give us someone who is practical and can pass the course.' The Sandhurst staff checked that I have O-level maths and then wrote the posting order that changed my life forever.

As I look more into the history of the role and my predecessors, I have a real sense of Kate passing the baton to me to run my leg of the equal opportunities race. She had made a fast start, as her tour had been very successful; it had to be, or the Army would not have considered raising the bar by allowing me to operate. When taking tentative steps in a new direction one wrong move could halt the momentum and the WRAC can't afford to make a mistake. Now it is down to me to build on the progress Kate has made and to take the next step on the road towards gender parity. I cannot afford to falter or fail. Any blunder I make will not only harm my personal career but will make it that much harder for any woman trying to become a bomb disposal officer in the future. If I get it wrong, I will

---

* Usually a lieutenant colonel for battalions and regiments.

90

turn out to be yet another obstacle to be overcome and not the springboard for those coming after me.

It has taken nearly fifty years for the Army to make a start but I am about to light that particular fuse. How will the public and rest of the Army react? I will soon find out.

5

Codes and Command

'I can't do this,' I concede reluctantly. I have absolutely no idea what to do next. I just never imagined it would be this difficult. It is my first day as a brand new 'fresh out of the packet' twenty-five-year-old second lieutenant in 33 Engineer Regiment (Explosive Ordnance Disposal), which is pronounced 'three three' and not 'thirty-three'.* I've been a commissioned officer for only two weeks, but Sandhurst seems a distant memory now. This is where I'll learn how to be a bomb disposal officer and I can't fail to be intimidated by the sheer size of the bomb that stands vertically just inside the camp gate of Lodge Hill Camp near Chatham in Kent, home of the EOD training school and my new regiment. The British 'Grand Slam' bomb that towers above me has a huge dark green warhead and a brilliant white tail the same length as the warhead; the notice underneath tells me it is a 22,000lb (10,000kg) earthquake bomb, the largest ever dropped by the British in World War II. At over eight metres in height, it is taller

---

* TV announcers and defence ministers take note as it really, *really* matters to at least get the bloody name right.

than my house! Earthquake bomb! What on earth have I let myself in for? I feel a little giddy at the challenge that lies ahead of me.

I'm met at the modern, low-rise, red-bricked Regimental Headquarters by the diminutive, smiley Adjutant, Nick. He is the senior captain and I'll be working closely with him. I'm pleased that he is a jolly sort, only a few years older than me, although he looks very boyish with a blonde turned-up fringe and a slightly lop-sided smile. He introduces me in turn to the Chief Clerk, universally known as 'Chief', a tall bruiser of a man sporting a spiky blond crew-cut, who will be my troop staff sergeant and my main colleague besides the Adjutant himself.

After I have been shown around the building and set up in my tiny Assistant Adjutant's office, barely bigger than the desk, with its connecting door to the larger, far more palatial Adjutant's office, it is tea-break time. At Sandhurst, we had been warned to be careful about making tea as some regiments seemed to think it was a 'woman's job', so we should only make tea for other officers and never for soldiers, as the male officers didn't do that. If we were in a meeting, it should be the nearest person to the teapot who is in charge of pouring drinks, so we should arrange to sit away from where the teapot might be delivered into the room, thus avoiding the whole 'Shall I be Mother?' tea-pouring situation. Nick asks me to make tea and coffee for the other officers so I can take it to their offices and introduce myself – this seems to fit within the WRAC guidelines for the politics of tea-making, so I am happy to do it.

'It's all laid out in the kitchen,' Chief says matter-offactly. 'There's a list of who takes what and the mugs are all labelled.' *Easy*, I thought.

And here I am, a few minutes later, utterly crushed, defeated. I cannot complete this, the simplest of office tasks – making tea. I need help. Yes, there is a list, but it reads:

CO: -2
2IC*: -1
Ops Major: C-, +2
Adjt: -1
QM: NATO

'What fresh hell is this?' I mutter.

I boil the kettle and lay out the mugs while I wrestle with the fiendish code. After ten minutes of struggling to make head or tail of it I finally accept defeat and resort to asking Chief for help. Across the armed forces of all the NATO countries there is a NATO Standard for everything and apparently the NATO Standard for tea is milk and two sugars, which is what you will be served unless you specify otherwise. Hence the Commanding Officer has tea with no sugar, the 2IC or Second in Command has milk and one sugar, the Operations Major has black coffee with four sugars (he's a busy man), the Adjutant has milk and one sugar and the Quartermaster has the standard milk and two sugars. Easy when you know what the code means, but I feel embarrassed and spectacularly pathetic after failing the first basic task of making a cup of tea.

---

* Second in Command or 2IC – in a regiment it is a major and in a company or squadron it is a captain. A deputy commander.

If I was struggling to make tea, how on earth was I going to pass a bloody bomb disposal course? Knowing that my predecessor, Kate, had passed the course was comforting to a point, but completing it knowing that I would soon be using the training for real was going to be tough. As I stand there fretting over the tea order my post is officially that of Assistant Adjutant, but I've hardly recovered from the shock of needing to be a qualified bomb disposal officer as well when I'm told that I will also be a troop commander of twenty-six male 'sappers' (as Royal Engineers are generally known) of Regimental Headquarters (RHQ) Troop. This is just as scary as being a bomb disposal officer. I had naively assumed that if I was to be a platoon or troop commander it would be a platoon of female soldiers or possibly teenaged Junior Leaders, but now I will have the far greater challenge of being responsible for twenty-six experienced combat engineers working in the Regimental Headquarters.

Initially, it seems like an overwhelming task to juggle all these roles (I am also the regiment's press officer) but it all quickly falls into place as I find out it's normal to have a variety of responsibilities within a military post. My troop are all clerks or storemen in the Headquarters, so I work with many of them during the day, and Chief is their immediate supervisor, which means that my role is to resolve any management issues rather than direct their tasks. I will be involved in their training, postings and promotions but I can do these things alongside my administrative role and apart from occasional inspections and troop nights out, I will meet them all for troop PT twice a week. Of course, all of this depends on me passing the bomb disposal course at the school next door when it starts in two months' time. If I fail, then I must pack up and leave on a new posting to God knows where.

By the time I arrive at the Headquarters I have already sewn the large red badge with a yellow and blue German bomb at its centre onto my uniform sleeve, as instructed in Nick's joining letter. It is very unusual for WRAC officers like me to wear any badges at all, given that they are mainly qualification badges, and at the time women are not allowed to join the infantry or corps directly, so our chances of gaining badges are pretty slim. Everyone in the regiment, whether they are trained or not, wears the sizeable bright red badge. Once they leave the regiment, those who are qualified wear a much smaller olive-green badge with the same bomb.

The red and yellow badge is a regimental battle honour granted by Queen Mary in 1940 and unlike some other badges, the bomb is worn on every form of dress, so if the Army ever issued pyjamas they would have a big glaring red bomb badge on them. The more formal the dress, the bigger the badge gets. On my formal evening mess dress the qualification badge is a gold bomb on a black background and it covers almost half my forearm! Subtle, it is not.

In my first week, Kate returns briefly to the regiment from her new WRAC posting to guide me through a few aspects of the job before I start bomb training in a couple of months' time. In smart civvies and wearing her long blonde hair in a pony tail instead of the usual bun, she looks calm and capable – the complete opposite of how I am feeling during this, my first week wearing officer's rank. She smiles brightly at the sight of my bomb badge. 'God, that's a fuck-off big badge. I'd forgotten the sheer size of it!' she exclaims cheerfully.

She advises me on how to handle the numerous press and media enquiries. I will need to deal with the usual local stories as well as the full-on *Daily Mail* bomb scare headlines because the regiment can be thrust into the limelight as the national main news item in a flash. I make copious notes as she passes on her experience of the regiment and we discuss the individual soldiers of RHQ troop who are now my responsibility. We say nothing about the bomb course, though, as there isn't much to say. Either I will be able to pass it or I won't.

During my second week I attend a WRAC Officers' Study Day where I am very self-conscious about my bright red stand-out bomb badge and the attention it brings me. Lieutenant Colonel Sally Bishop, the Commander WRAC for South-East District, stops me in the foyer. While being very supportive, she brings home to me the fact that the eyes of the whole Army, as well as those of the WRAC, are on me. Her parting shot rings in my ears: 'Just pass the damn course,' she asserts.

A career as 'Officer in Charge of Earmuffs'* in some remote and dusty storeroom would surely be my fate if I let everyone down now. The stakes are high, not just for me personally but for all serving women looking for equality progress. They are counting on me to get it right. No pressure then.

★

---

* Term for the most boring and inconsequential job imaginable.

Before I begin my training to become a bomb disposal officer, I focus my energy on being a female troop commander of an all-male troop and frankly it has its challenges. In common with Kate, I don't take myself too seriously so the light-hearted banter with the troop is refreshing and fun. They are happy to welcome me into the fold so I begin to feel more at ease in my new surroundings. During my first week, I join the troop for morning PT which, naively, I am looking forward to. As I am fresh out of Sandhurst I consider myself quite fit, but I am seriously deluded. Troop PT is twice a week before work, so we meet at the gym at 7 a.m. for a run. We form up in a squad with the officers from Headquarters at the back but they set off at a pace that is the speed of my flat-out sprint, so I am out of breath, have turned purple and am struggling to breathe by the time we reach the camp gate. I have never run with a male squad before and their stride is much bigger than mine, which really doesn't help. By the time we have run from the camp down to the Medway shoreline I want to be sick. Running along the wet sand, I *am* sick. I am so slow that when they run a mile or so along the waterline the rest of the squad have to keep doubling back to pick me up again. Everyone else does press-ups and squat thrusts while they wait for me to catch up. I am exhausted and deeply embarrassed, it is so humiliating. Running uphill on sucking wet sand is a killer and after an eight-mile run I am practically crawling, with my lungs burning and my legs feeling like lead.

I decide that I must up my game and so I am determined to get fit enough to keep up with my troop. Within six weeks of extra early morning runs and heavy gym sessions in the evenings I am able to overtake a couple of the slower soldiers, who are then screamed at by the PT staff for having the audacity to let a woman get in front of them. 'Call yourself a man? Are you going to let a *woman* get in front of you?' screeches the PT corporal in the ear of the poor soldier as I flail past him. One corporal, who I regularly work with, asks: 'Ma'am, would you mind awfully not running so fast as I much prefer the press-ups to the grief I get when you overtake me on the hills.'

On the Commanding Officer's Run, which is a compulsory eight miles, the Regimental Sergeant Major tells the regiment that any man passing the finish line after him would be required to parade wearing a skirt. I make sure that I finish ahead of him.

My regiment, 33 Engineer Regiment (EOD), shares its living accommodation with the Royal School of Military Engineering at the bottom of the hill, about a mile from the Regimental Headquarters. As most of the officers in the mess are students on various courses and not permanent staff, the arrangement is that 33's officers will live in shared houses or mess annexes just outside the back gate of the Engineering School, so that they don't feel as if they live in a hotel. This means that I will share a three-bedroomed semi with the female WRAC lieutenant working at the Engineering School, so at least I'm not the only woman here and will have a more experienced friend to guide me in my new life. The male troop commanders from 33 live in the house next door, so we can socialise easily after work. I'm immediately welcomed into their circle.

After eight weeks of settling into both the house and

my role as Assistant Adjutant and troop commander, the day finally dawns for me to begin the long-awaited seven-week bomb disposal course at the tri-service Defence EOD School (DEODS), which is inside Lodge Hill Camp, next door to the regiment. It is co-located for practical reasons: the Army staff at the school will be recruited from the regiment and the regiment's officers will often need to refer to munitions in the DEODS Technical Information Centre or museum. I'm going to need to be as familiar with Napoleonic cannonballs as I am with Soviet missiles or naval torpedoes. All three armed services train here in both EOD and high-risk search and the current commandant of the EOD School is a Royal Navy lieutenant commander.

Thankfully I will be living in the same shared house as before, so the only change is turning left inside the Lodge Hill Camp gate to go into the school instead of right into the Regimental Headquarters. Adjutant Nick has banned me from coming into the office until I have finished the course. I'm allowed to attend social events such as the upcoming Regimental Ladies Dinner Night but I'm absolutely not allowed to do any work or be distracted by thinking about what's happening in the regiment when I should be concentrating on being a good student.

The course joining instructions tell me that it will run from 08.30 to 17.30 unless we have practical sessions, which are likely to overrun if we need more time. There are no classes at the weekends but there will be lots of homework and private study. After the long working hours of Sandhurst this seems practically part-time so I'm delighted that

I can go home at weekends to see my family, even if I have to work while I'm there.

The course students assemble at the EOD School on the first day and I'm thrilled to discover that I'm not the only woman, as there is a female RAF officer too. 'Morning!' she says with a relieved smile as soon as she sees me. 'I'm glad I'm not the only one.'

'Me too!' I say, trying desperately to remember what the RAF ranks and their Army equivalents are. She is wearing two light blue bands on her jumper epaulettes and I haven't a clue if that means I have to call her Ma'am or not. I should have listened to the RAF lecture at Sandhurst rather than nodding off in the warm lecture hall. I only have to salute majors and above (unless it's an Adjutant and everyone salutes the Adjutant at the start of the day).

Luckily the first activity is registration and I discover that she is a flight lieutenant, equivalent to an Army captain, so I can call her Jackie. In fact, of the thirteen of us on the course there are only two from the Army, me and a Royal Engineer warrant officer joining my regiment as a squadron sergeant major. All the others are RAF, mainly flight sergeants with a couple of flight lieutenants. The RAF has only one dedicated bomb disposal unit (now disbanded) and none of the students are going to that unit, so only the warrant officer and me will be operational. The flight sergeants are armourers who deal with the explosives in ejector seats and may need to remove unexploded bombs from a crashed RAF aircraft, so bomb disposal falls within their remit. The officers are their supervising engineering officers who need to know the theory more than the practice. This is just a tick in the box for them. Their career stream means they need the qualification but they are unlikely to ever put the knowledge gained into practice, whereas I will definitely be operational once I have qualified and these skills will save my life. This places us poles apart.

When I was at Sandhurst I learned about fighting a conventional war against the Soviet Army, which realistically was never going to happen (the Berlin Wall had just fallen and the Soviet military threat was collapsing fast), but this course is different as I will soon be using these skills for real and could be making life or death decisions at the end of it. This thought focuses my mind so I vow to pay attention to every word, ask questions, do my homework diligently and become a 'girly swot'. Like the Royal Engineer warrant officer, whose reputation and standing are at risk if he fails, I also stand to lose a lot. I'm now feeling increasing pressure because if I fail I will then be posted out and not replaced, so it will be the end of female bomb disposal officers and it will be all my fault. In my gut, I know that failing is not an option and this is going to help me focus on the challenge ahead.

On our first day, after the usual preamble of registration, we are introduced to our instructors. They are mainly Royal Engineer warrant officers who have been selected for their teaching skills as well as their extensive bomb disposal experience. I know from the last two months that these are highly regarded experts who are so well respected that if I impress them I will be accepted as an equal by the rest of the regiment. Up until now, I feel as though I've been welcomed on a temporary basis and given the benefit of the doubt until I've passed the course. I need to prove my worth.

As the most junior officer and the only Army one I feel quite exposed; there is a certain distance among the students. The officers are largely unsmiling and I wonder if they volunteered for this or if it is an unwelcome distraction, but I'm so junior and not in the same service, so maybe that's the reason. I just don't have the military experience to tell the difference. The flight sergeants are definitely more approachable, although I am shocked to see that one has a beard – something that is strictly forbidden* in the Army as it prevents an air-tight seal on our respirators.†

The female flight lieutenant, Jackie, has a very severe short haircut and the bearded flight sergeant asks me quietly: 'Would the Army let you have a haircut like that?' He was clearly disapproving.

'I don't think Sandhurst would like it much, but I doubt that anyone else would actually say anything,' I reply. 'Maybe in some regiments, but not mine,' I add, thinking of the misogynistic hassles that some of my Sandhurst friends have had in their new units. I have escaped any sort of conflict with my all-male unit. 'The RAF seem more relaxed about things like that,' I say diplomatically, as we are joined by his friend, another flight sergeant, who has a bushy droopy moustache and glasses that darken in bright light – both no-no's in the Army. We are carefully avoiding calling each other anything at all, as no one is

---

* Goat majors (again – don't ask) are allowed beards as are Sikhs.

† Gas masks.

quite sure of the correct protocol between classmates with different ranks. It is my first course after Sandhurst so I will wait and see how this unfolds before using first names with anyone other than the officers – Jackie, David and Graham.

After the introductions it's straight on to the first subject – explosions and explosives. No surprise there. It turns out that there are mechanical, atomic and chemical explosions – so far so good. Despite my less than extensive scientific knowledge I can follow the explanations and I make copious notes. As I catch a moment to cast a glance at the rest of the class, I notice that the RAF engineering officers don't make notes but nod knowledgeably. With no questions at this stage, the burly instructor, Staff Sergeant 'Sandy' Sanderson, with his broad smile and easy manner, moves on to the two types of chemical explosives: high explosives and low explosives.

Low explosives exert a lifting and pushing force, are easily set off by heat or friction and burn rather than explode if they are unconfined. This means they are used as propellants or incendiaries, so a rocket will be launched by a low explosive that is directed and controlled. I draw a firework to remind me of the push, the burning and the ease of ignition with just a match. I look up and see that all the RAF students are making notes now.

High explosives cut and shatter, rather than push. They are divided into: primary explosives, which are very unstable and highly sensitive to shock, heat and friction, and secondary explosives, which have a complex molecular structure, are less sensitive and can only be detonated by using a primary explosive. As the instructor talks expertly through the slides and diagrams I embellish my notes by drawing a detonator, which is a highly sensitive primary explosive inserted into a stick of plastic explosive, which is a secondary explosive. You can set off a detonator by a flick with a fingernail, apparently, yet you can hit plastic explosive with a hammer and it won't go off. I decide to take his word for it.

The final section illustrates the effects of explosives; blast, earth shock, fragmentation and incendiary. All the different ways they can kill you. Lovely.

By the end of the first day my head is swirling with new terminology, 'speed of velocity' numbers and the use of additives for tweaking the power of the explosions. I've learned that powdered aluminium is added to the explosives that are used in underwater weapons like torpedoes to increase the gas produced, so that the explosion will lift the ship and break its back.

There is just so much to take in that I go straight back to my shared house and spend the whole evening writing up the key points as neatly as I can. After my wrist injury my handwriting is all but illegible (like a three-legged drunken spider crawling off the page to die, according to one instructor) and I really need to be able to refer to these notes later. W.H. Smith do not stock revision guides to bomb disposal so I will need to rely on my handwritten notes.

I turn up to the school on day two to find that the Royal Engineer sergeant major is arriving at the same time. His textbooks, waterproofs and notebook are in a camouflage-patterned backpack that is near identical to the one over my shoulder. He salutes and smiles broadly, stretching the neat grey-flecked light brown moustache that frames his mouth. 'Glad to see that the Army is on time, Ma'am,' he jokes, as I return his salute. We are both twenty minutes early.

We go through our notes from the day before and ask each other a few questions to make sure we have both understood it all correctly. Although we maintain the usual rank distance and do not use first names we will work closely and look out for one another throughout the course, not least because we have the honour of the Army to uphold. We may even work on the same bomb together in the future, so we learn to trust one another.

The flight sergeants bundle into the classroom as a group, very upbeat. After spending some of the evening in the bar of the Sergeants' Mess they are beginning to feel more comfortable in an Army environment. They are carrying their books in sports bags; the sergeant major catches my eye and raises an eyebrow in disapproval. The bearded one, Roger, and the man with the dark glasses, Bob, are already friends from past postings and they come across to sit with the sergeant major and me. After last night's chat to my more experienced WRAC housemate I decide that I can call the flight sergeants by their first names, as we will never meet again professionally so there is no chance of making the mistake of being over familiar in a more formal setting. The flight sergeants use the sergeant major's nickname of 'JJ' and try to avoid calling me anything in company, but when we are alone they call me Lucy. The officers turn up last but are not technically late; they are living in the main Officers' Mess, which means that our paths will rarely cross outside the school. The mess is at least a mile away so they have brought packed lunches and will study while they eat at lunchtime.

The second day focuses on pistols and fuzes. I keep very quiet so I don't show my ignorance as I realise that a pistol is not a gun and a fuze is not the same as a fuse. Apparently a fuze contains its own explosive charge to set off the main bomb and a pistol is basically a firing pin inside a case. Again, I draw illustrations in the margins of my notes to help me understand the implications. At breaktime the two flight sergeants, Roger and Bob, grab a coffee from the vending machine and sit down with JJ and me. Roger is tall and bespectacled but with appallingly misaligned teeth.

'RAF dentist?' jokes JJ.

'Junior rugby,' Roger laughs, rubbing his ginger beard to reveal gaps among the crooked teeth.

'I'm more of a football man,' says the far shorter Bob with a twinkle in his eye, which disappears as soon as his glasses darken again. I find the ever-changing glasses very distracting.

Turning to JJ he asks: 'Who do you support?'

'Umm, I prefer cricket,' says JJ, killing the conversation. A conversation that I had been unwittingly excluded from by their body language, lack of eye contact and minimal expectation of women's interest in predominantly male sports. There's a brief pause, so I fill the awkward gap by asking Bob if he's grasped the morning's topic. I then feel a bit of a fool as I remember he's an RAF armourer, so will know all about bomb pistols. Bob's now in his element as he explains that you can't put a fully live bomb straight onto an aircraft – the risk of an accident is too great. Any detonation on the ground would destroy a number of aircraft and possibly wreck the runway too and detonation while flying in formation would wipe out the other planes. Therefore the bomb has to be unarmed or deactivated with a safety device when loaded and travelling inside the plane but live when it hits the target. Somewhere in between the plane and the ground it needs to become armed.* That's where the pistol comes in.

That all makes sense, so JJ and I nod to show that we're with him so far. The bomb can be armed electronically after the bomb bay doors open when approaching the target, but it may have a pistol that uses arming vanes like mini propellers. As the bomb is released the vanes rotate freely in the airstream and after a pre-set number of revolutions a striker is moved into line with the detonator inside the bomb, so it becomes armed well away from the bomber that dropped it. 'Aah,' sighs JJ, understanding. 'That's why there are so many unexploded bombs around; if the plane was flying too low then the bomb wouldn't have time to arm so it lands without exploding,' he says. Roger and Bob nod in agreement and I add drawings of a falling bomb to my notes, vanes turning as it drops.

The afternoon's sessions move on to Soviet bombs, which are much less interesting for me – none had been dropped on the UK (yet) although our current and future enemies are all likely to use the same basic designs, even if they weren't bought directly from the Russians. The images and diagrams show us the key parts of any bomb regardless of who dropped it: there's a stabilising design feature, usually fins at the back to make sure it lands nose

---

* Ready to explode on impact.

first, lugs to attach it to the aircraft and a mechanism to detonate it. While German bombs have fuzes on the side of the bomb casing, others have fuzes on the nose or on the tail – some are designed to explode on the surface or, in the case of a 'bunker-buster', once they have gone deep underground. I'm going to have to learn to deal with every type from every nation and the scope of this is rather overwhelming.

By day three, the pace is picking up and our broad-shouldered instructor, Staff Sanderson, is clearly talking about his pet topic: Land Service Ammunition – the military term for projectiles, mortars, mines, pyrotechnics and grenades. That is, virtually everything not dropped by an aircraft. As he waxes lyrical on the basic designs of his favourite mines and grenades, we can't fail to notice the badges on his jumper. He wears the small green and yellow bomb qualification badge on his forearm as well as a gold old style diver's helmet badge with the gold letters SW, indicating that he is a shallow water diver skilled in underwater engineering. He also wears paratrooper wings on his shoulder, so he only needs the commando dagger badge to make the full 'boy scout' set. Only the bomb badge can currently be worn by a woman. It would be another thirty years before women could wear the others.*

Once the classroom theory is over, we troop outside and cross the car park to the EOD Technical Information Centre, which is packed with examples of every type of

---

* The All-Arms Commando Course was passed by Captain Pip Tattersall in 2019; Captain Rosie Wild passed the famous Parachute Regiment All-Arms P Company Course in February 2020 and collected her wings in September 2020.

bomb, mine, mortar and explosive item we might ever hope to find. We're here to look at perfect examples that will help us recognise the corroding versions out in the field. I pick up a plastic NATO anti-tank mine and turn it over in my hands – the first touch of a mine, albeit a deactivated one.

'Lucy!' an urgent voice calls. 'Come and look at this!' It's David, one of the RAF officers, who is beckoning me over to something on the other side of the mine display in the main hall of the museum. I walk towards him and stop, aghast. There in front of me is a green-painted original German World War II V-2 rocket. The V-2 is an enormous beast of a rocket. It is nearly 46 feet (14m) high and it weighs 27,600 lb; if ever there is a symbol of the devastating power of the explosives dropped on Britain then the V-2 is it. The V stands for *Vergeltungswaffe*, meaning 'Retribution Weapon'. I stare at it in awed, horrified silence. The sight of this breathtaking bomb, tall enough to nearly touch the hall ceiling, brought home the enormity of the challenge ahead. My father was bombed in London during the war and both of my parents were evacuated away from bombs like this one, never thinking that their daughter would one day be responsible for making them safe. I stand there mesmerised, for longer than I realise. I can't take my eyes off it.

6

Is It the Black Wire or the
Brown Wire?

Once out of the classroom at the end of a long, intense day the students on the bomb disposal course scatter in all different directions: the RAF officers walk to the Officers' Mess; the flight sergeants to the Sergeants' Mess; JJ, the Royal Engineer, goes to his sparse, empty married quarters, where his family will join him once he's passed the course and knows he can stay; while I go to my shared house outside the barracks wire. There is only a narrow, fence-lined one-mile-long route between the accommodation and the bomb school at the end of the no-through road, so anyone on that isolated thoroughfare is an obvious terrorist target, with no means of escape. Following the teaching that was drummed into us at Sandhurst, I avoid setting a predictable pattern by setting off at varying times and rotating between walking, driving and cycling; that's all I can do to protect myself. Bomb disposal officers are high-value targets for terrorists and it's ironic that, right now, while I'm learning my trade with inert bombs, the most dangerous part of my day is the journey to and from work. A few days before I started this course an RAF corporal and his six-month-old baby daughter were both shot dead by the IRA, who lay in wait at a petrol station, so the risk is real and the stakes are dangerously high.

Over the next couple of weeks, the classroom lessons continue with guided weapons – the next evolutionary stage from the iron bombs that are simply dropped in (hopefully) the right place. I make lists of all the ways in which the missiles, rockets and bombs can be guided to their targets; how they find their target will determine how we can approach them. For example, a laser-guided missile usually has its target acquisition system in the nose, so we should approach it from the tail to avoid it 'seeing' us and detonating. A crashed, unexploded infrared missile could detonate if it mistakes the heat signature from my body, contrasted against a cold night sky, for the intended target. I hadn't even considered the possibility of having to hide from an unexploded bomb and then trying to sneak up on it undetected before attempting to make it safe. The RAF students are more familiar with air-to air missiles and runways are key targets for guided weapons, so they are very attentive listeners during these lessons. The officers ask lots of technical questions but JJ and I are more unsettled by the sheer range of ways in which we can be killed when tackling them.

After a couple of weeks, we have completed enough of the theory of all things that go bang to be able to put our wellies on and head outdoors to put some of this newfound knowledge into practice. As at Sandhurst, I again have problems with kit not being female-friendly, but this time it's the wellies. Just trying to find black Army wellies that fit me is a real challenge. Men's boots start at size seven, so I have to cadge a pair from the Queen's Gurkha Engineers in Maidstone, as they are the only unit that stocks boots small enough to fit my size six feet. It's a small hurdle but that doesn't make it any less frustrating.

The grounds of the DEODS bomb school are a rundown area of slightly overgrown grassy patches interspersed with small areas of hard standing and four black, corrugated steel Nissen huts used as workshops. Scattered across the area are a quantity of rusting bombs, mines, mortars, missiles and all manner of mystery objects.

'Welcome to the recce circuit,' announces Staff Sanderson, spreading his arms wide to show the extent of the military scrapyard around us. 'What I want you to do is to get into pairs and work your way around this numbered circuit. Try to identify what each of the munitions or bombs are by looking at the design features, such as fins and fuzes, we have covered this week. Keep some distance apart so one pair starts at Item Number One, one pair at Item Number Ten and so on. Keep going around until you have all identified every munition on the circuit.'

David, one of the flight lieutenants, makes a beeline towards me saying: 'As you're Army I reckon you'll know more about mines and mortars than the others.' I hate to remind him that I'm fresh out of Sandhurst so my knowledge of this stuff is pretty non-existent. He looks a little disappointed as I tell him that he should have picked an old hand like JJ if he wanted genuine knowledge rather than guesswork, but we're paired now so we decide to make do. We head off to the first bomb together to decipher the clues armed with a notebook and a tape measure. I peer at the rusty tin can at my feet and David squats down to take a closer look.

'Well, it's got fins so maybe it's air-dropped, but it's quite small,' he says.

'No lugs or anything attached to the sides so maybe not,' I say, picking it up and turning it round to see. 'Ah, hah!' I exclaim. 'Holes in the tube attached to the fins – it's a mortar!' I declare, following up with: 'Mortars are shells dropped onto a firing pin so have fins to stabilise them.' I'm ridiculously pleased with my first diagnosis; mortar bombs are a common infantry weapon, with the bomb being lobbed high in the air and coming down at a very high angle. They've been around for hundreds of years and I know the regiment deals with thousands of them.

'Number Ten is a two-inch mortar bomb,' says David; he writes it down as I measure the width of the rusty metal.

'Right! On to the next!'

Slowly we work our way round the lumps of rust, checking details such as the tell-tale signs of an artillery shell – a copper band around it that is scored with grooves if fired or smooth if not. Slim missiles are air-to-air anti-aircraft weapons as they are already at altitude when fired, while fatter ones are surface-to-air or surface-to-surface as they need more thrust to reach height, so they have bigger rocket motors. We also have to recognise half-exploded devices, so the inside of an anti-aircraft missile resembles metal bands that fly in all directions when detonated, piercing the fuselage of a plane. Even a single part of a bomb can indicate what has happened. Staff Sanderson tells us a story about a chap mentioning that a small bomb landed in his garden during the war and made a small crater, the only thing left of it being a large steel ring. It was the Kopf-ring that was added to the nose of a 1000lb German bomb to prevent it penetrating too deeply into the London clay. The crater was the entry hole and the live bomb was still under his back door. Over the coming weeks we would return to this recce circuit many, many times as it is so important to correctly identify what you are dealing with. As we were all painstakingly aware, any mistakes in identification could be fatal.

On this first visit, though, David and I have come up with a few certain identifications and a few guesses, but one in particular has us stumped. A tear-drop shaped bomb that is obviously old but in relatively good condition.

'It's definitely air-dropped,' says David, 'judging by the big fins on the tail.'

'But no lugs, just a metal bar at the very back behind the fins,' I shrug, baffled.

Staff Sanderson comes up behind us. 'That's a handle at the back,' he said, trying to give us a clue, but we're still none the wiser. 'It's an early Zeppelin bomb from World War I – you just open the window of the airship and drop it out!'

Blimey.

The following week, the course continues with a mix of classroom, workshop and outdoor activities and now that we are feeling more confident about the types of explosive weapons we are introduced to the first piece of bomb disposal equipment – a metal detector. 'This is a Foerster

Locator 4021,' announces Staff Sanderson, as he points to the large green box beside him. 'It looks like a croquet set,' mutters one of the flight lieutenants. We are once again in the outdoor area behind the school, but this time we gather beside a giant sandpit that has lanes marked with fluttering white mine-tape.

Staff Sanderson opens the box to reveal a cable, metal poles, a small electronic box and an earpiece. The box has a moulded interior that holds each item in place, including six slots for the batteries. Not only do we need to know at a glance if anything is missing but we may have to build the locator quickly in the dark, feeling for each section in turn. He kneels to construct the locator and talks us through each piece as he expertly slots it into place. This is the Army way of teaching: clear step-by-step instructions with a practical close-up demonstration. Once the locator is built the experienced instructor holds it up and takes us through the checks and tests to make sure it is working correctly – lives will depend on it.

'How come it doesn't look like a normal metal detector, with a round plate on the end to sweep across the ground?' asks Bob. This is something we have all been thinking as we look at the strange arrangement. A vertical pole hovering a few inches above the ground is connected to the front of an electronic box, which is then connected to the horizontal metal pole in the instructor's hand. 'Oh, we have those too,' says Staff Sanderson, 'but we use those for detecting mines and small items of ordnance that are close to the surface.' He points to a stack of large green boxes beside the sandpit. 'You're going to be playing with those this afternoon, digging up whatever you find, but this is a locator which operates to a far greater depth and its readings will not only show you where a large bomb is but also the angle at which it is lying within the ground.'

This time I am paired with ginger-bearded Roger and between us we manage to build and test our locator quickly, talking our way through the sequence and watching each other's hands to reinforce the learning. If any step is missed the other person will spot the error before we go anywhere near a bomb. Once Roger and I have the locator correctly set up we learn to plot the readings it produces from boreholes as we search for buried bombs in the sand, one inch at a time. We spend hours training on detectors and locators to find mines and buried bombs, trying to make sense of the readings by working out what an object is and where it is before digging it up to see if we are right.

During the afternoon Staff Sanderson chats to JJ and me, who will both be operational with the regiment at the end of this course. 'There are eighty-nine abandoned unexploded bombs in London at seventy-four sites that we know of,' he says. 'They are on land which will never be developed so they are quite safe, but we have to re-plot them every so often as they can "walk". The London clay shifts and shrinks in times of drought so the bomb can change position or be pushed higher over time. You may be involved in the re-plotting so it's good to see that you've both grasped how to do this so easily.'

As I finish plotting the last of the large bombs deep under the sand, I have a sense of immense satisfaction. I feel that I've been coping well so far and I don't seem to need as much help from the instructors as some of the others, which is a good sign. I'm finding the tasks fascinating and the instructor thinks I'm doing OK; I really need to hear this as next week we move to the chemical phase of the course, which I suspect will be my weak spot. Chemistry was my least favourite science at school and according to the timetable chemical weapons are a key element of this course.

Most of the EOD students go home at the weekends so I alternate between going home to my parents and spending the weekend in the shared house, hanging out with the male regimental officers next door. It is lovely to hear the regiment's gossip again and find out how my troop are getting on, so I feel I have a foot in two camps. I also have someone to ask if I'm struggling with my homework.

One Sunday afternoon I'm relaxing with my WRAC housemate in the boys' house next door; we are watching *Zulu* – yet again – one of the classic films enjoyed for decades by junior Army officers. We all know the script so we're chatting over crisps and beer as we watch. Suddenly there is a loud beeping sound in the room. The lads clap and cheer as Ben slops his tea, leaps up from the sofa and grabs the Duty Bomb Disposal Officer's pager on his belt. He reads it carefully and dashes to the phone to call the Operations Room. Someone has found a bomb! One day very soon that could be me, I think, as he runs out of the door and jumps into the white Land Rover with its red wings and blue lights, on his way to make an unexploded device safe.

The chemical phase of the bomb disposal course starts with a shock. Within the first lesson it becomes clear that

I am expected to be the battlefield expert on chemical weapons! I will need to be able to plot chemical bomb locations then calculate the width of the gas cloud and the downwind vapour hazard as the toxic gases move across the battlefield. Then I have to warn troops in the danger area. Despite their use in armed conflict being banned by international law, those nations that wish us harm all have access to chemical shells, bombs, rockets and missiles. Even after the 1982 Falklands War, leaking Argentine napalm shells were dealt with by Royal Engineer bomb disposal officers and chemical weaponry has spread since then. This is a huge responsibility, as hundreds of lives will depend on my calculations of air temperatures, wind speeds and the nature of the chemical agent. I'm determined to get to grips with this weapon of mass destruction.

I begin the heavy task of learning the gruesome ways in which the various types can kill you. Nerve agents such as Sarin, VX and more recently Novichok, as used by Russia in Salisbury, interfere with messages from the brain and so paralyse the muscles, causing you to suffocate. Add to this the blood agents, the choking agents and the blister agents and then the different ways to detect and neutralise them and it all seems overwhelming. I am already aware of the blister agents such as mustard gas used in World War I, because canisters are regularly found in the UK by the regiment. Mustard gas shells were stockpiled in World War II in case of a Nazi invasion but never used, so many of them ended up being buried. I decide to start with mustard gas and work my way down the list.

Although most of this phase is theoretical, there is a practical element: wearing a bright yellow gastight suit

over our breathing apparatus so we can detect the chemical agent and tackle leaking chemical munitions. The gas
suit resembles a baggy romper suit, which I find extremely
claustrophobic, and my mask fills so high with sweat that
if I lean forwards to look down at a bomb I have to look
through the swishing salty liquid to try to see what I am
doing. With my vision a blur, the deepening puddle in
the mask tickles my eyelashes and stings my eyes. None of
this discomfort is helping as we struggle to deal with the
chemical shells. The instructors are not surprised when
all of us fail to plug the leak in a cracked mustard gas shell
using plaster of Paris bandages. There must be a better way
as this all seems very futile. God help us if the next war is
a chemical one.

JJ turns up in the classroom early one morning and
proceeds to unfold a massive sheet of coloured squares. 'I
made a chart,' he says, looking dolefully at the complicated
connections between chemical agents and the corresponding chemicals we must use to neutralise them. 'I thought
using colours would help me remember what goes with
what,' he says. 'But it doesn't really.'

'I know,' I say sadly, unfolding my own complex chart
of coloured blobs. In the end we resort to making a
matching card game similar to Snap and we play it every
morning while we wait for the RAF students to turn up.
Slowly the information sinks in.

The rivalry and banter between the services flows thick
and fast, as it always has, particularly between the RAF
and the Army. The RAF was formed on April Fool's Day,
partly from the Air Battalion of the Royal Engineers, so

it started from there. RAF personnel are paid more than us and never like us to forget it – they wave £20 notes at us and ask if we've ever seen one before. They are also prone to leaving us a 50p tip, telling us to go and treat ourselves. On the course, the one woman and the ten men of the RAF contingent taunt us by each wearing different uniforms every day and mixing up the forms of dress, as well as making sure that no two of them are ever dressed the same. This is deeply distressing to us Army folk, who collectively don our jumpers on 1 October and take them off on 1 May, regardless of the temperature, just to ensure we all look the same. As a sergeant major, poor JJ takes it very personally and has to grit his teeth whenever he sees an RAF person with no hat on or wearing a blue shirt with a green jumper. Eventually the RAF students confess that they do this deliberately just to irritate us. Bastards.

After the intense chemical phase we move on to learn radiography, as we will need to X-ray home-made letter bombs and pipe bombs. My confidence returns for this element as I have been looking for bomb components on airport X-ray scanners for years as an airport security officer. It takes some practice to recognise everyday items on X-ray and I am able to help the others interpret what they are looking at among the different shades of grey on the X-ray plate. One letter bomb we X-ray contains parts of a disposable lighter which, to the instructor's surprise, I spot instantly (they're not allowed on planes, so I'm tuned to recognise them). Even Staff Sanderson listens carefully as I explain that a lead crystal bowl contains lead so although it looks like glass in your hands, you can't see through it on the X-ray.

★

One week we finish early, picking up our homework at 2.30 p.m. on the Friday and heading off for the weekend. I'm staying in Kent this weekend as tonight is 33 Engineer Regiment's Ladies Dinner Night in the mess, my first formal dinner night and only the second outing for the horrendous 'curtain' that is my WRAC mess kit. This time, though, I have the new bolero mess kit jacket in dark green with gold trimmings, so I feel more glamorous than ever before. I make quite an entrance among the smartly dressed wives of the regimental officers and a major's wife comes across to me to admire my jacket with the bomb badge glaring on the forearm. She explains that she used to be a WRAC captain and hated the ugly curtain, so she thought this was a massive improvement. 'You look as smart as the men now,' she says approvingly.

As the most junior officer present I am 'Madam Vice', sitting at the far end of the table, and my role is to respond to the toasts. Once the port is poured (from the left, never leaving the table) the Second In Command stands and announces: 'Madam Vice: The Queen!' I then stand to say as clearly as I can: 'Ladies and Gentlemen: The Queen!' and we all stand to make the first toast. By the time we've toasted the Engineer-in-Chief and God knows who else I really want to sit down. I'm engrossed in conversation with one of the majors when I'm aware that people are leaving the table. Since no one is allowed to leave until the official end of the dinner, I assume that the formal part is over and I carry on my conversation. Only later in the bar do I realise what has happened. The ex-WRAC captain sidles up to me and says: 'Well done, I love what you did back there, so cool, so smooth.' I look confused; I have no idea what she's on about. 'Umm, sorry, but you'll have to explain, it's my first real dinner night and I'm not sure I understand.'

'When the Commanding Officer's wife gets up to leave after the toasts, that's the signal for the ladies to withdraw for coffee and leave the men at the table with the port to talk shop,' she explained. 'You just glanced up at us leaving and carried on talking about Ben's bomb last week; this is how it ought to be when women do the same job as the men. Good for you!' She gives me a big smile and returns to her husband at the bar. I am a little dazed that I have just set an important precedent without even knowing anything about it.

Back at the bomb school on Monday morning, Friday's dinner night is farthest from my mind as my class of would-be bomb disposal officers studies electrical circuits. JJ is on familiar ground here as he reveals that he is a qualified electrician. 'It's been a while, mind. I'm a bit out of practice but the basics are all there,' he grins. He seems relieved that his existing skills give him some welcome breathing space. The course is very demanding and an easy section helps balance those sections where everything is totally new.

After watching a blur of wiring diagram images on the classroom screen I'm given an array of wires and components, with the instruction to make a variety of firing circuits that will light up a small torch bulb if built correctly. I work hard to complete the first circuit, then I test it – nothing. I go back to check the connections to try to find the fault, but the bulb stays stubbornly off. Hmm, I think, which bit is wrong? I glance up from my desk to see JJ waving a small transistor at me. Aha! I alter the connections on my transistor and lo! – I have light.

Once we have all cracked the desktop circuits we go outdoors to practise the upscaled versions and spend what seems like days winding the two-core black and brown twisted firing cable onto large drums after each practical session. This cable is what we use to fire the ring main that allows us to set off multiple explosions in sequence. The instructors are very particular about how the cable is wound – it must be under slight tension and evenly spaced across the reel and David and I find ourselves doing it over and over again. He holds the cable taut while I turn the reel and we smooth the cable across the surface. 'How much is it costing the defence budget to have two officers spend hours winding this bloody cable?' he moans.

'I dread to think,' I agree. 'But getting it right must be important or they wouldn't make such a fuss about it,' I say. We finally get the nod from the instructor to show he is happy with the standard of our cable.

'If there's a nick or a fault in this cable,' the instructor says, 'you will have to go out into the open and repair it or replace it, surrounded by enough explosive to remove you from the face of the earth. And very possibly under enemy fire as well.'

'OK,' says David, as he reaches for the next reel, 'he's got a point.' When we connect detonators and charges with this cable of black and brown wires twisted together, Staff Sanderson insists that we must connect the brown wire first *then* the black one if we are Army, but we must connect the black one first if we are RAF. This seems very odd, but it gives us something to think about while we work. It helps us to keep focused and doesn't allow the mind to wander during the routine stages of bomb disposal preparation. As I connect the wires, I mutter to myself: 'I'm Army so brown wire first – done! – now the black wire.' I'm concentrating on getting each step right every time.

Once I've grasped the electrics, the next stage is sensitive detonators: slim metal tubes either fired electronically or with a fuse cord. Here we listen carefully to a new warrant officer instructor who has a mangled, scarred left hand. Nobody likes to ask how his hand got into that state as the ugly repair looks quite new, but the other instructors watch him closely from the doorway as he explains: 'Hold the detonator between your fingers like a cigarette, with the tip furthest from your hand, partly to avoid the heat of your hand and partly so it reduces the chance of losing more than a couple of fingers if it goes off.' He is demonstrating with his right hand as his other hand doesn't have enough whole fingers left. You can hear a pin drop in the classroom as we watch transfixed. He goes on to teach us that detonators can be set off electrically by pressing a button on a shrike, which is essentially a big switch, or alternatively by using a black powder fuse very similar to that used in cartoons by Wile E. Coyote to blow up the Roadrunner. You light it and walk away, it fizzes along its length to the detonator and the heat then sets it all off. It works underwater too – much more fun than just pressing a button. Bob and I cut lengths of safety fuse and predict when the detonator will fire. There is a great satisfaction in being able to count down smoothly to an explosion.

'Three, Two, One, Firing!' Bang!

Standard military plastic explosive or PE4 is an extremely stable high explosive with a consistency similar to marzipan or modelling clay, so you can mould it. High explosive moulded into a V shape will cut steel in two, so we practise the effect of different shapes. It comes in the form of a white stick wrapped in an innocent-looking white wrapper and it's easy to cut through with a knife. Roger cuts off half a stick of PE4. 'I'll just use this,' he says, grabbing a wine bottle from the array of objects we could use. 'The neck of this will give a good cone shape to focus the effect; anti-armour weapons have cone-shaped charges inside.'

'You'll do better with a metal object,' Bob says, picking up a metal angle bracket and offering it to Roger. 'That way the metal becomes a molten slug to punch a hole through the steel.'

'You're both right,' says Staff Sanderson, nodding. 'A copper cone shape can penetrate armour or at least cause a massive metal scab to peel off the inside of the tank and fly around at speed, killing the crew.'

We're consistently reminded that we can never escape the death aspect to all this. Once we have practised preparing charges there are lessons on countermining, which is to place an explosive charge next to, but not touching, a UXO (an unexploded munition, so smaller than an unexploded bomb). When we detonate our charge, the shock wave will also detonate the UXO and destroy it – all without anyone touching it. We watch as a small amount of explosive detonates in the open air, barely making a mark on the ground and doing little damage to objects around it, but the same couple of grams of explosive, if confined inside a container, will be many times more powerful, making a crater and damaging the surroundings. This is what makes buried bombs in Afghanistan so deadly: the blast is concentrated and forced upwards. JJ and I plan to create battlefield obstacles by blowing up trees with detonating cord; wrapping the cord round the trunk and exploding it. There is even explosive squirtable foam to blow a padlock off a gate. So much fun! As I learn more each day my confidence grows and while handling the explosives and detonators becomes a familiar task, I still talk my way through what I'm doing so I get each stage correct.

While most of the course was completely new to me, I found one section easier than the others – tying knots and working with ropes. A key principle of bomb disposal is to do as much as you can remotely, to avoid putting yourself or anyone else in the danger zone. A couple of days of the course are therefore taken up with learning to use the Allen Hook and Line Set, which is a suitcase full of pulleys, clips, ropes and hooks. Once we've mastered some basic knots and attached pulleys and clips to the right place, we can take up a safe position behind something solid and then, with one heave of a rope, lift a car's door handles and pull the doors open remotely. Being able to move something remotely is not just safer but it could also make the task easier. For example, if the fuze on an iron bomb is underneath we have the option to either dig under it and work on it upside down, which will limit our

choice of method, or use ropes and pulleys to rotate the
bomb from a safe distance, so we can access the fuze easily.

At the time, in 1989, the main terrorist threat comes
from the IRA. One month before my course started, the
IRA used a time bomb to blow up the Royal Marines
School of Music in Deal, killing eleven Royal Marine
musicians. Our training, therefore, focuses on their tactics
and favourite devices. The IRA favour hiding weapons
and bomb-making components inside a plastic dustbin
that is then buried deep in the woods somewhere. The bin
will often be booby-trapped, so we need to be able to pull
it out and then empty it beside the hole without standing
anywhere close. We learn to use lashings to make a large
tripod over the site of the bin and then hoick it out using
hooks and ropes. After that, we can make it bounce around
and tip out the contents, carefully avoiding dropping the
weapons back down into the hole. All those hours of knot
lessons aboard the tall ship *Zebu* really help me on this
phase, so I find it interesting but quite easy.

As the weeks of training go by, it slowly dawns on me
that we are never going to be given a step-by-step guide
to bomb disposal. Since every situation is different, we are
being taught various techniques that might be applicable
to the circumstances around us and we are being shown
how to use equipment such as X-rays, so that when the
time comes we can choose for ourselves which piece of kit
might help and how we can approach the problem. While
there are Render Safe Procedures* for certain stages, such
as immunising the fuze of an iron bomb, there is no set

---

* A laid down plan of how to deal with a particular stage.

plan for dealing with every device – this is hugely disappointing to me as I have naively been hoping for a tried and tested plan that I can follow step-by-step, but now I realise that I am going to have to make it up as I go along!

7

Ticking Timebombs

It's four weeks into my bomb disposal training and I am being dragged along the rough ground on the end of a rope tied around my waist. I get snagged on a tussock and then I'm yanked free and hauled to safety. The rope is the final safety measure to retrieve me or my body from the danger area around an explosive device.

I'm wearing a bomb suit for the very first time and I quickly discover that it isn't designed for women. It really doesn't fit the female form and particularly not mine. Even though I'm slightly taller (and wider) than the average woman the chest plate is too long, so it hangs down well below my hips, which prevents me from sitting down or kneeling properly. It is also too wide, so my arms stick out like a dingly dangly scarecrow and when I bend forwards it overlaps and locks against the groin plate, so I just topple forwards and head-butt the practice rocket I am trying to deal with. The weight of it then slumps me sideways and I can't manoeuvre either my arms or legs underneath me to get back up again. I flail around like an upside-down beetle doing backstroke before suffering the indignity of having to be dragged back to the safe zone by Roger and

Bob, hauling on the rope tied around my waist. It's neither successful nor safe.

Bomb suits aside, if you are going to indulge in a particularly hazardous activity it makes sense to have a serious conversation with yourself about the risks you are willing to accept, so that you can then put it all out of your mind and be at peace to get on with the job. The risk of injuring other team members is minimised if the most dangerous stages are carried out by one person alone, the Number One. Lying awake worrying, or dwelling on all that you stand to lose, is not helpful preparation for the day ahead. Dealing with a viable explosive device requires focus and absolute concentration, so a nagging worry about the consequences of a wrong move is a serious and unnerving distraction.

In the early weeks of my bomb disposal training on the Explosive Ordnance Disposal (EOD) course I get together over a few drinks in the Officers' Mess bar with my fellow officer students, Jackie, David and Graham, and the cheery subject of death crops up. It is obviously something on all of our minds right from the outset – the death rate and average life expectancy among bomb disposal officers (BDO) on operations has never been the most attractive part of the job. In World War II, the life expectancy of a BDO was just ten weeks and things didn't improve after that. During the 1982 Falklands War, the casualty rate was 100 per cent. Two Royal Engineer EOD operators were defusing an unexploded bomb (UXB) on board HMS *Antelope*, one of the frigates providing air defence to the beachhead in San Carlos Water, when it detonated, killing the Number Two, Jim Prescott, and maiming the Number

One, John Phillips. So the risks are genuine and deserve some reflection and perspective. My main attitude is one of simple, blind denial – it won't happen to me.

Given that we cannot normally choose the timing of our demise, the conversation revolves around what type of death we would opt for if we could choose the *manner* of our deaths. We all agree that the ideal death is to die at home, while snoozing in front of the fire after a delicious Sunday lunch, when we are spritely ninety-four year olds (or thereabouts). Since the job we are about to undertake considerably lessens the chance of this happening, we consider the next best option. After airing our worries (hands shaking, mind going blank, etc.), we come to the conclusion that a 'good' death has to meet three requirements. It has to be:

1. Instant – going from full faculties to stone dead in a heartbeat. It avoids the dreaded steady downward decline into frailty.
2. Painless – an obvious condition for the perfect death.
3. Unexpected – not knowing that you are about to die. This is *very* important.

We then compare different possible military deaths. Your parachute not opening scores points for the first two elements, for example; one inch above the ground you are absolutely fine – on the ground you are definitely not. So the instant part is a tick. Painless? Yes, we assume hitting the concrete at 120 miles an hour would be so fast that it counts as painless – tick. The problem is that the unexpected element – the panicked seconds of struggling to get a reserve chute open or desperately trying to untangle the lines – is distinctly undesirable. It's the same problem if you are stuck in the path of an approaching tank; a tick for the first two but a fail on the third. After a few more drinks we come to the conclusion that the sudden detonation of a large bomb we are working on ticks all the criteria of a perfect death, even if it comes seventy years too soon.

A Sandhurst cadet tasked to write an essay entitled 'What is Courage?' once wrote 'This is.' and handed it in. It was not well received. Courage, whether it is physical or moral courage, is overcoming your fear and finding the strength to do what you least want to do. Fear is a spectrum. On the one end, it's exhilarating – it's like the popularity of horror films and lengthy queues for the white-knuckle rides at expensive theme parks. You've seen the people in front of you get off the ride safely. They are fine, they are laughing with relief and exclaiming 'It was so scary!' and 'I thought I was going to die. I want to do it again!' It makes you feel alive. On the other end of the spectrum is the blood-chilling, bowel-liquidising certainty that it is *not* going to be all right, that you *will* die without a miracle – your parachute has not opened/is on fire/you simply haven't got one. If you live, you will never *ever* want to do it again. Bomb disposal lies somewhere in between.

My Army training does not stop me from being scared but it teaches me how to react under that stress. When faced with a frightening scenario, some people may become frozen and paralysed with fear – a bunny in the headlights, unable to do anything but stay and wait passively for disaster to hit them between the eyes. Rigorous Army training teaches you to use that same fear to motivate yourself, to use the fight-or-flight reflex of adrenaline to boost your resources, to act and not freeze and to push yourself onwards to do things you didn't know you were capable of until that moment.

There is, however, also the constant, underlying strain that comes from working in bomb disposal every day. I find that the best tactic to deal with this type of stress is to deny to myself that what I am going to do is in any way dangerous: *Just a short walk, lift this, tighten that, put that there, press this button* – all completely out of context. Say it in your head in a sing-song voice and it turns into nothing to be frightened of. It's easy to become paralysed by the fear of making a mistake or its consequences. As Staff Sanderson keeps reminding us: 'You can make all the mistakes you like, just not *the* mistake, and even if you do make *the* mistake and it goes bang, then you won't hear it, feel it or know anything about it and will certainly not get into any trouble afterwards, so just don't worry about it.' I cling to this belief as my way of processing the risks I am running and it works; so long as I can kid myself that it will be instant and painless, I can sleep soundly, even when much later, after passing the course, I am the Duty Bomb Disposal Officer on call waiting for my pager to go off, summonsing me to action.

This belief works for me right up until 30 July 1990, when Ian Gow, the Tory MP, is murdered. On this day, the IRA planted a sizeable bomb under Ian's car outside his home, which detonated as he manoeuvred the vehicle out of the carport. He suffered the classic catastrophic, unsurvivable injuries that are the result of a Semtex Improvised Explosive Device (IED) placed directly under the driver's seat, but sadly he did not die instantly. He knew exactly what had happened, remained conscious and spoke to his wife, living for at least ten minutes after the blast before succumbing to his dreadful injuries.[*] From that moment on, I could no longer pretend to myself that any fatal mistake would be swift and painless.

It is not just MPs at risk, though. In the late 1980s and early 1990s, nowhere is safe if you are in the Army. The Provisional IRA is just one of a number of groups seeking to murder service personnel. The risk of being killed by the IRA or any of the other terrorists when off duty is very real – probably higher than being killed at work. The year 1990, which begins a few days after I complete my training, is a particularly bloody year outside Northern Ireland, with a number of bases and recruiting offices being bombed and all ranks targeted; the Air Chief Marshal is shot nine times in his Staffordshire home[†] and a young soldier is shot dead at Lichfield train station. Bombs exploding in England, including in the Stock Exchange, are a weekly event during that summer. Even two Australian tourists are killed in the Netherlands after being mistaken for British soldiers. The military police in Germany are all armed whenever on duty and patrols are supplemented by Auxiliary Military Police drafted in from other regiments, also armed.

By the time I'm training as a bomb disposal officer I am

---

[*] *Eastbourne Gazette*, 1 August 1990

[†] https://publications.parliament.uk/pa/cm199596/cmhansrd/vo960304/text/60304w13.htm

aware of the dangers of being in the Army and even before I joined I was exposed to the harsh realities of military life. The recruiters had suggested that I go on a familiarisation visit to a regular barracks to get a better idea of what life as a WRAC officer might entail, so they arranged for me to visit Inglis Barracks in Mill Hill, London. This base is home to a large number of WRAC servicewomen as it is the Depot of the Army Postal Section, a branch of the Royal Engineers.

I catch a train to Mill Hill shortly after a fatal bomb attack on the barracks by the Provisional IRA in the summer of 1988 and I am shocked to see that an entire two storey barrack accommodation block has been completely destroyed, killing a young soldier as he slept. The parade square is still cordoned off, so my small group of fellow potential recruits has to walk round the debris of the destroyed roof that has been blasted across the barracks. This is the sobering reality of Army life – the ever-present threat from terrorism. We are all made acutely aware of the risks of a career in the military, not just serving in operational theatres doing dangerous jobs but here at home, in London, while we sleep.

During my training, like most service personnel, I take a number of safety measures such as changing how I travel to work. I walk, drive or cycle in no particular order, as well as varying the times when I set off – anything to break a predictable pattern. I check under my car carefully and run on different routes, making sure that I have no regular routines – thirty years later I still do this by using different car parks, etc. Almost unconsciously, I never set a pattern of action where I can easily be intercepted. By becoming a bomb disposal officer I have added to my risk and deliberately, publicly put myself in harm's way by taking a new step forward for military women.

One way to lessen the risk when on duty is to wear a bomb suit, but the benefits of wearing a suit are rather limited in 1989. The heavy Kevlar suit, with its large chest plate and smaller groin plate, is designed to protect the user from the shrapnel propelled at close range by a small device like a hand grenade. The sacrifice for this protection is overheating, cumbersome weight, restricted movement, a steamed-up visor and a higher centre of gravity. It will not protect me from the overpressure of the blast wave, which will damage the lungs. This pressure wave can do more damage than shrapnel to soft, squishy humans. Besides that, it stinks to high heaven, so no amount of Chanel No. 5 is ever going to make an impact on it. Although the suit might protect me from something the size of a grenade or possibly while I walk towards the bomb, if I am dealing with a World War II bomb that is the weight of a Volkswagen there really is no point in wearing it. For us, the only advantage of wearing the bomb suit is that it enables you to be buried in a shoebox instead of in a matchbox. It saves on the tidying up too, apparently . . .

Staff Sanderson and his fellow instructors continue to introduce us to different bits of kit and let us work out the best way to use them in various situations. Occasionally we work with a piece of equipment that can only be used in a certain way and only applies to a limited range of devices; an example of this is the microphone stethoscope, which listens for ticking bombs (yes, really). The ticking of a clockwork fuze, to be more precise. This came as no surprise to any of us as we'd all seen the popular 1979 TV drama *Danger UXB* and the *Dad's Army* episode that involved ticking bombs. Some of the World War II German fuzes were electro-mechanical clockwork fuzes, which created a delay between impact on the target and the bomb detonating. Once the bomb hit the target, the electrical fuze fired a thermite pellet which melted some wax pellets, thus allowing the clockwork mechanism to start ticking.

The clock on a Type 17 fuze could tick for anything between two seconds and seventy-two hours before detonating, so when we are working on an iron bomb we learn to attach a microphone stethoscope with a long cable. The Number One bomb disposal officer and their Number Two can then hear if digging up the bomb has restarted the jammed clockwork timer.

'Each time you carry out an action on the bomb you should stop and wait a "soak time", sometimes just ten minutes, sometimes two hours, to see if your action has activated the mechanism,' Staff Sanderson explains. 'If you ever hear ticking in your headphones or your Number Two shouts "TICKING!" as you are working on a bomb, you should take the appropriate steps, which are bloody big ones, as fast as you can, in any direction you like,' he adds cheerfully. As the timer could have jammed with only a few seconds left to run I hope that I'm not next to the bomb down a deep hole at the bottom of the ladder when that happens.

Other equipment is rather less specialist, such as the remote camera called a Jack-In-A-Box that we set up close to the bomb to film any action we carry out, so if we make a mistake that detonates it, the next person facing a similar device will not repeat our fatal error. Personally, I'd prefer not to make the mistake in the first place.

We are occasionally left to learn from our mistakes. I am paired with David, one of the RAF officers, and we are getting to grips with how to use a rocket wrench. Some bombs have fuzes that protrude from either the nose or the tail and these have to be unscrewed and removed, but as we try to do everything remotely from a safe distance we use a gadget. A rocket wrench is essentially a metal clamp with two small explosive cartridges attached to it that fire in opposite directions to rotate the wrench. First the wrench is securely clamped onto a protruding fuze and it is then fired electrically (using the black and brown twisted firing cable) to make it spin like a Catherine wheel and unscrew the fuze from the bomb, while we watch from a safe distance. So far so good, but after our first attempt to remove a tail fuze David points out: 'The fuse is now unscrewed all right, but it is still in the end of the bomb. We've somehow got to pull the damn thing out.' I grovel in the toolbox and produce an elastic bungee cord, which I hook on to the wrench and loop around a stake hammered into the ground, so it will pull the fuze clear of the bomb as soon as it has sufficiently unscrewed. 'That should do it!' I say, feeling very clever as I return to the safety area.

David calls the warning: 'Firing now!' He presses the button on the electronic shrike which completes the circuit and fires the cartridges in the wrench. There is a loud pop and a whizzing sound as the wrench spins fast, but the bungee becomes twisted tighter and tighter as the wrench rotates. It tightens so much that it doesn't just pull the fuze out but it catapults it back towards us at speed! Staff Sanderson turns his back on us, but we can see his shoulders shaking as he chuckles at our rookie mistake.

On our next attempt, David twists the bungee in the opposite direction to the rotating wrench so it unwinds as the wrench turns. That part works fine but when the fuze pops out it hits the stake holding the bungee cord, so it would have detonated anyway. Eventually we learn to place both ourselves and the stake at an angle to the bomb and successfully remove the fuze smoothly every time. The instructors could have told us how to do it correctly the first time, but we learned so much more by finding out for ourselves. I feel elated at the achievement and decades later I can still remember how to use a rocket wrench.

Once we've understood many of the techniques and been introduced to most of the equipment by practising on inert bombs at the bomb school, the time has come to practise on live bombs. For this we need to move to the live ranges out on the Essex coast.

The military training area of Shoeburyness is home to miles of empty mudflats that are used as demolition ranges at low tide. As we stand by the trucks waiting to drive us across the hard mud to the demolition area, Graham, a flight lieutenant, looks out to sea and says: 'I wonder if we can see the masts of the *Montgomery* from here? I've always wanted to see it.'

'And what is the *Montgomery*?' asks David. I'm glad he did, as I've never heard of it either.

'The SS *Richard Montgomery* is an American munition ship that ran aground and broke open in 1944, just off these mudflats. It's still got about 1400 tons of high explosive on it and it's so dangerous that there is a permanent exclusion zone around it. If it went up – well, let's just say I wouldn't want to be anywhere near here,' explains Graham.

'So why haven't they dealt with it before,' I ask, 'if it's so shallow you can always see the masts?'

'They did try to clear another ship in the sixties that only had a fraction of the explosives on board and was nearly four miles offshore but it exploded with the force of an earthquake measuring 4.5 on the Richter scale, so God knows how big the explosion would be if the *Montgomery* went up,' says Graham, clearly pleased he knew something that we didn't.

'Well, since it's below the highwater mark it clearly belongs to the Royal Navy, so they can deal with it,' says David. 'Just as long as it doesn't go off while we're out here on the mudflats,' he adds. 'If we survived the blast, which is highly unlikely, then we'd drown in the tsunami it would create.'

'Oh, thanks for that thought, David,' says Graham sarcastically, rolling his eyes at the rest of us. 'That's just what we need to hear while we're setting up live thousand pounders.'

Out on the mudflats, far from the shoreline, we practise setting light to safety fuses.* Every reel of safety fuse has a

---

* Devised by Englishman William Bickford for use in mining, it was originally gunpowder wrapped in a rope covering that burned slowly to allow miners to move to a safe distance before the main charge detonated.

slightly different burn time, so first of all we need to cut a foot length and time how long it takes to burn. Then we can calculate the length of fuse needed for us to get to a safe distance. Although military safety fuse can burn underwater that could affect the timing, so it ought to be kept dry if possible. As the retreating tide has left pools of water everywhere, we push wooden posts into the sandy mud and tape the fuse to the top of them to keep it dry. Once we know how much fuse to use, we can begin the serious business of rupturing 1000lb bombs and torpedo warheads. The fuzes have been removed so we are faced with safely disposing of the main charge of high explosive or rocket propellant. The objective is to destroy the bomb by exposing and burning off the explosive content without it 'high-ordering', or exploding with its full force. JJ and I are wearing full military kit with our neat berets and soldiers' black gloves, whereas the flight sergeants wear bobble hats, baseball caps, mittens and all manner of jumble. Some things don't change.

One method of rupturing a bomb casing and burning the contents is to fire a shaped charge at it. A cone-shaped layer of copper is detonated from the rear of the cone, which then melts to a liquid and forms a slug of molten metal that hits and pierces a small area of steel plating. Shaped charges are powerful enough to cut steel as well as penetrate tanks. We need to improvise this effect so we make a Baldrick device, which is a metal tube with a two-pence piece at one end. A detonator is used to fire the coin at the bomb casing, which causes the two pence to become a slug of molten copper capable of blasting a hole through the steel casing and setting light to the explosive content – all without detonating it. With only a small amount of explosive, we can make a large bomb safe.

We take turns to be the main operator, the Number One, with the rest of the small team helping to set up the fuse. The day is spent placing charges and lighting the fuse, then jumping into a large red-painted Bedford truck (red so it is easy to spot against the brown mud) and driving a safe distance to watch through binoculars for a small tell-tale puff of smoke and steam that means the bomb has been cleared safely. We pelt back across the wet mudflats to examine the red-hot burning bomb casings and look at the resulting steaming crater. It is deeply satisfying to be able to blow up 1000lb bombs rather than the smaller munitions we have been working on so far. We can only use the furthest ranges if there are no low clouds, as the blast could deflect off the cloudbase and then break all the windows on the seafront just across the water. My small group begins to get quite competitive with the timing of the fuses, to the extent that whoever was the acting bomb disposal officer (BDO) for a particular bomb owes the rest of the team a pint for every second they were out with their timing. After three hours' practising I am owed a number of pints and my slate is still clean so I'm feeling smug. David is seriously out of pocket and beginning to get grumpy.

As the day on the ranges draws to a close and the sky grows darker, we quickly set up the final test firing, which is to be my last one as acting BDO. The tide is beginning to come in, so we are paddling around the rocket trying to keep the fuse out of the water. The rocket is not the actual warhead but the rocket motor, which is a solid propellant that will only partially detonate if I rupture the casing. The truck's engine must be running before I can light the fuse, just in case it fails to start, so with the truck idling I light the fuse and check it's burning properly. Then we leap into the back of the truck and speed through the shallow water to the safety point. Once there, I count down to detonation: 'Three, two, one, firing!' Nothing.

David, Bob and Roger cheer and start counting pints excitedly as the seconds tick away. I check with my binoculars but there is no small puff of smoke to show it has fired correctly – in fact, I can't see the rocket motor at all. I drop the binoculars and realise I can't see it because of the massive mushroom cloud that is rising high into the sky. The twinkling lights of the town across the water disappear behind the enormous explosion of the rocket motor high-ordering, or exploding with its full force. In fact, it shouldn't have made that big an explosion even if it had fully detonated. A pressure wave thunders across the mudflats, pushing the tide in front of it. We feel rather than hear the crack of an explosion which shouldn't have happened, followed by an echo as it rebounds off the cloud base. I don't hear much as my eardrums have burst. We are all safe, although wet and rather deaf.

Unbeknownst to any of us on the mudflats, the final rocket motor was a different type to the ones we had been working on all day. This one had a special lining, which not only meant it couldn't rupture in the same way but also meant that the propellant was confined, so the pressure built up until it high-ordered – and with even more force than the amount of explosive would usually produce. I never did find out how we came to be given the rogue rocket motor, but I did realise how easily things can go wrong even when practising in peacetime – we were very lucky not to be seriously injured and luck plays a big part in my chosen career. But in keeping with the 'it won't happen to me' mindset, I try not to let it throw me and continue to focus on the job.

8

Rockets and Robots

Once back from the excitement and drama of Shoeburyness Range we return to Staff Sanderson's classroom in
DEODS bomb school for lessons on nuclear bombs and
warheads, which cover both fission and fusion devices as
well as issues with 'dirty' bombs, which are linked to terrorism. A 'dirty' bomb has no nuclear explosion but uses
a conventional explosive to scatter radioactive nuclear
material, contaminating a wide area.

Our theory sessions cover not just the actual bomb but
how to reach it by digging shafts or pumping out water. JJ
reassures me that the rest of my team are combat engineers
who have spent years practising this, so I only need to
know the process at this stage. Sometimes getting to the
bomb is harder than making it safe. Just three years earlier,
in 1986, a 500kg German World War II bomb was discovered under forty feet of water inside a large gasometer in
Beckton, East London. The bomb disposal team of three,
wearing diving gear, were lowered down through the poi-
sonous fumes from the top of the huge metal collapsible
tank. Then they dived to the bottom of the toxic water
to attach lifting tackle and lifted the bomb into a rubber

dinghy, before defusing it by torchlight. Having safely defused it they then had to get it out through the hole in the top of the gasometer, a hundred feet above them, before lowering it to the ground to be steamed out by the rest of the team. All three men, an officer, a staff sergeant and a sapper, were awarded the Queen's Gallantry Medal. Big shoes to fill and here's me thinking that defusing the bomb was going to be the hard part!

Luckily, I am paired with JJ for the next subject: building and services protection. As an experienced sapper with construction trade experience behind him, he is already familiar with much of this topic.

'All the evacuation distances are based on wartime calculations relating to pre-1930s buildings, which are mainly made of brick,' explains Staff Sanderson, pointing to the charts in our text books listing the size of bombs and the corresponding evacuation radius. There are three columns: Complete Evacuation, Partial Evacuation and Windows Open. Opening all the windows allows the pressure wave to pass through the building without damage. In April 1992, a large home-made IRA bomb detonated outside the Baltic Exchange building (now the site of the Gherkin) in London and caused £800 million worth of damage (equivalent to over £1.6 billion in 2021). The Baltic Exchange itself was an older building too badly damaged to save and the steel-framed, glass-fronted buildings in the whole area were extensively damaged by the blast due to their construction. 'We need to move the evacuation cordons wider to reflect the extra flying glass and less absorbent steel of modern buildings. Also, timber-framed houses can't withstand blast in the same way as a nineteen thirties brick house,' he continues, 'so take a good look around you before deciding on the radius of the cordon.'

It's not just the construction materials that make a difference; we learn to put sandbags in cellars to absorb the ground blast or the house will shift a couple of inches sideways on its damp course. Ground shock from a bomb detonating can crack water pipes or fracture the gas main so the lessons cover how and where to dig protective trenches to vent this ground blast, stopping further damage and complications. We are advised to use whatever material is to hand to create protective walls that will minimise damage to key points.

I look at the extensive list of evacuation distances and realise just how big an operation defusing a large iron bomb can be. No wonder there is always a Duty Field Officer to help turn off the gas, stop the trains (a passing train causes its own ground shock so could shake a jammed timer) and divert overhead aircraft (blast goes up a greater distance than it passes through the ground). There are just so many factors to consider besides the actual bomb!

There is one type of bomb that particularly excites the RAF students far more than any other, and that is a runway denial bomb. It takes the form of a two-part dispenser: one part contains thirty small bombs that could penetrate the runway's hard concrete, producing craters; and the second part consists of up to 215 bomblets or cluster bombs (anti-personnel mines*) that scatter around the craters, exploding at random or if disturbed. The aim is to prevent the runway from being repaired so that aircraft are trapped

---

* Now unlawful under the Land Mines Treaty.

on the ground while returning enemy bombers attack the airfield.

Initially JJ and I relax, as this is clearly an air force problem and so not one for us. The RAF officers Jackie, David and Graham argue over the best way to deal with the cluster bombs.

'You could just bulldoze them out of the way,' suggests Graham.

'But the shaped charge in the bomblets would wreck the bulldozer, so you've just blocked the runway even further,' argues David, 'and lost a bulldozer that you need to fix the craters in the runway!' he adds. There's a silence as we all ponder the tricky problem.

'What about using high pressure hoses from the fire appliances to blast them out of the way?' proposes Jackie. Nods of agreement all round.

'Yes, that is certainly one way of moving them, but it doesn't stop them going off intermittently, which would restrict the repair work on the runway,' interjects Staff Sanderson.

'You won't have long before the bombers are back, so the quickest method is to shoot them with one of these,' he continues, as he presses the button for the next slide on the screen, which reveals a massive rifle. 'The fifty calibre Barrett sniper rifle. If you were shot in the chest by this it would cut you in half – from a mile away.' Staff Sanderson pauses to let that fact sink in.

'We mount it on a tripod so you have a good chance of hitting the bomblets without being a skilled sniper,' he says.

He doesn't know just how bad I am at shooting, I think

to myself, remembering my appalling scores at Sandhurst. Just as well this is largely a problem that affects RAF airfields.

During the course I come across a technique that enables people to concentrate on a single task – something that's invaluable when you're working in bomb disposal. It's best explained by imagining this scenario: if someone asks if you can hear an odd noise, we automatically mute some of our senses in order to boost the key one we need. To better hear a noise, we look down at the floor as that is the least visually stimulating background, but our eyes are kept open as this helps us identify the direction of the sound. We fix our unfocused gaze to avoid unnecessary visual input and our breathing rate slows along with our heart rate as we quieten our body and shut it down to concentrate on listening. Cold, hunger and any other distractions momentarily disappear as we zone in on the single simple task. We hold our body completely still so the brain can burn brightly, focusing on picking out the various background sounds and then discounting them. It usually takes seconds before we decide that we can't hear the sound in question at all or that it is the fridge next door buzzing. I discovered that I can hold myself in this highly alert yet partially shut down state for a prolonged period and think fast while carrying out a single focused task – an essential aid to passing the most challenging test in my end of course exams: the critical fuze immunisation test.

One type of bomb that I'm actually looking forward to dealing with is a World War II German iron bomb and all attention now focuses on how to deal with these.

'This is one situation where there are laid down "Render

Safe Procedures" and we'll go through your options and cover fuze immunisation in detail, as you will be tested on this in the final exams,' says Staff Sanderson. 'All nations marked their fuzes clearly to show the armourers which type it was,' he continues. The RAF students are all nodding – this is their day job. 'German fuzes all have numbers stamped on the head of the fuze, like this,' he says, as he flicks the next slide on the screen to show a round aluminium disc on the side of the bomb casing. It resembles the top of a Coke can – this is the fuze! In the centre there is a raised circle containing the heads of two copper plungers. Among the letters and digits stamped around the top of the fuze is a circled number 15, showing it is a Type 15 fuze.

'Back in 1940, an electronic fuze could be "switched off" by short-circuiting the electric charge that fires it, then pulling the fuze out of the pocket that it sits in on the side of the bomb,' Staff Sanderson continues. 'So the Germans added the ZUS 40 anti-withdrawal fuze underneath the main fuze as a booby trap, as well as changing the electrics to detonate if short-circuited, so that stopped us taking fuzes out.'

'Bastards,' says JJ.

'Quite,' responds Staff Sanderson. 'They even devised a Type 50 fuze which only armed the bomb long after it landed, so it was specifically designed to kill bomb disposal officers – just a tap with a pencil was enough to detonate it!' The room is silent. This is a deadly game of cat and mouse from decades ago that we are still playing today.

Modern iron bombs may contain battery-operated fuzes, so in one of the Nissen hut workshops we learn how to use liquid nitrogen to freeze and kill the batteries. David and I mould a clay dam around the fuse while Graham and Bob prepare the liquid nitrogen and pour it into our dam until a few centimetres of frost appears on the surface of the bomb.

'It takes a couple of hours, so you need to test how far the freezing has spread. Put balls of wet cotton wool on the bomb and when they freeze onto it then you know it's working,' explains the instructor. Just when we think we have mastered this technique the instructor spoils it by reminding us that it only works if the fuse is on the upper side of the bomb, so we may have to rotate the bomb. 'There must be an easier way,' says Bob exasperatedly; he had really struggled with the ropes and pulleys.

Having learned the freezing method, we troop back to the classroom to learn the current method of immunising a World War II iron bomb fuze. 'After all these years the charge in the condensers has dissipated but the picric acid inside the fuze has combined with the corroding metal to form picrates, which makes the fuze very sensitive to shock or friction.' Staff Sanderson pauses to check that we are all following – this is important. We are all glued to the image of the fuze head on the screen and hanging on his every word.

'In other words, it's still going to go bang if we move it; we can't pull the fuze out so no point in freezing it – so what do we do?' asks JJ.

'We use this,' says Staff Sanderson, pulling out a tiny woodworking hand drill that reminds me of the hand whisks in school cookery classes.

'Seriously?' I ask.

'Yes, absolutely. You're going to drill into the head of the fuze, screw in a hollow needle, attach a plastic tube, create a vacuum then introduce a bottle of saline solution and pressurise it with one of these,' he smiles and flourishes a bicycle pump. Once the RAF contingent stop laughing, he continues. 'You pressurise the saline solution within the fuze to make sure it reacts with all of the picrates and you wait an hour or more while it desensitises them to immunise the fuze. Once the fuze is immunised you can move the bomb to a better location, where you're going to use a trepanner* to cut two big holes in the casing, steam out the soluble TNT or Amatol explosive onto hessian sacking, then set light to it.'

There's no laughing now – just a moment of stunned silence before the questions start. Once we've immunised the fuze the bomb is safe to be moved and other people will get involved. The regiment has a team of sappers on stand-by called the Crash Crew, who deploy to help us dig down to a bomb as well as carrying out the trepanning and steaming. The next few days are spent learning to get the immunisation procedure right, then using the massive trepanner, which clamps onto the bomb to cut through the steel casing. Staff Sanderson recommends cutting a hole near the tail as the casing is thinner there. We watch the ancient-looking steam boiler in action. The long hose snakes across the grass to the bomb, with the nozzle end in one hole as the now liquid explosive content bubbles harmlessly out of the other. Staff Sanderson points out the sharp axe lying close to the steamer. 'If the boiler ever

---

* A trepanner machine makes a wide hole – like an apple corer.

breaks down and stops steaming you'll need to use that to cut the hose a bit sharpish or the explosive could get sucked back up the hose and into the boiler, where it could go bang.' I make a note to stand near the axe but away from the dodgy looking steamer. It looks more dangerous than the bomb.

We're now coming towards the end of the bomb disposal course and it's the IEDD Phase, or Improvised Explosive Device Disposal – the terrorist bomb or the home-made booby trap. Retreating armies often use booby traps to delay the enemy from following them; to distract them; and/or to deny them the use of abandoned equipment. The methods are not that dissimilar to terrorist devices, so they detonate when someone enters a building or touches something, although booby traps usually utilise military munitions such as a grenade. A glass coffee jar balanced on the top of a half-open door can be made deadly by placing a fragmentation grenade with the safety pin re-moved inside it. When the door is opened the jar falls and shatters, releasing the lever that detonates the grenade inside. It is quick to set up and uses easily accessible com-ponents. Larger devices are made by using artillery shells, mines or other munitions as the main charge to be set off by the victim.

In order to clear IEDs I need to be able to think like the bomber – what do I want the victim to touch? Where would they stand? How can I catch them out? To make a device that detonates when it is moved I use mercury tilt switches that I can adjust to give different sensitivities. A small blob of mercury inside a sealed glass tube rolls down the tube as it is tilted and completes the circuit when it bridges the terminals at one end. The IRA used to acquire these from vending machines, as they set off an alarm if you tilt the machine more than a few degrees. I could set them up to detonate the bomb if you move it just five degrees in any direction.

The only limit to IEDs is the imagination of the bomber – there are just so many ways to die. An IED can be detonated by the victim – by picking up a torch for example – by a chemical reaction such as sulphuric acid in a condom that slowly dissolves until the acid comes into contact with an incendiary or by someone watching with a remote key fob and pressing the button to send a signal when the victim is in range. An IED can also be detonated by a collapsing circuit if a wire is cut. Sneaky doesn't cover it: other detonation methods are a photoelectric cell in a dark cupboard, so it goes off if you shine a torch on it or open the door, or pressure pads under the carpet near a door or window. The list of 'how' is endless.

We do, however, have various tools at our disposal; letter bombs are often light sensitive so they may only detonate if you open the envelope but some have thin wire which is pulled as you draw out the letter, so the solution is to X-ray them before deciding how to tackle them. We have extensive ECM (Electronic Counter-Measures) or jammers to block signals from mobile phones or key fobs while we work.

As with conventional bombs, the rule is to do as much remotely as possible to reduce the risk to the bomb disposal officer. Bob and I use a weight-dropper, which is a gadget that looks like a sack barrow but which will drop a heavy sandbag from around waist height when you pull a rope. I remotely drop the sandbag onto each floorboard rather than step on them. It takes ages to make progress into a room but it saves accidently stepping on a pressure plate and it is a lot less messy to clean up.

Among the tools used by bomb disposal officers for dealing with devices remotely is the famous Wheelbarrow robot, as seen in any film or TV programme where an attempt at realism is made. The Wheelbarrow is a small tracked robot which can be mounted with cameras and various weapons to deal with devices from a safe distance. One key weapon is a sawn-off shotgun loaded with grape-shot. This can be fired at car windows to break the glass so the robot can move forwards and use its camera to pan around and search the inside of the vehicle. The black and white camera is limited on the earlier models and has no depth perception, so as we're practising with it in the car park it keeps bumping into the device.

'Why don't we stick a flap of black gaffer tape on it, which we can see move a fraction when it arrives at the device,' suggests David. The Army is entirely held to-gether with black gaffer tape, so this is just another use for it. Bob is having too much fun driving the Wheelbarrow and won't let anyone else have a go, so Roger resorts to pulling the cable out of the control panel until he agrees to share it nicely. JJ and I enjoy firing the weapons on it more than the driving aspect, but that's probably why we're in the Army and not the RAF.

The Wheelbarrow is also fitted with a disruptive weapon. This is essentially single-barrelled, like a shotgun, but it's fired electrically and can be loaded with a variety of cartridges. Newer developments include firing scalpel blades to cut wires remotely.* There are different calibres of barrel, from a small 'needle' for letter bombs to a large 'hot rod' for car boot devices. The main cartridge we use in 1989 is a shot of water which, when fired at velocity, tears the device into pieces without it exploding. Firing a disruptive weapon is what is known as a controlled explosion. Unless you are unlucky enough to hit the detonator, there will be a small bang as the disrupter is fired and the device is made safe. It has the advantage that water doesn't remove fingerprints and since none of the components have been totally destroyed it is possible to gain all the vital forensic information.

While this sounds like a very useful tool to have in our arsenal, Staff Sanderson repeatedly warns us not to rely on the Wheelbarrow as all specialist kit would undoubtedly be destroyed on Day One of any conflict while we struggle to tackle an overwhelming number of unexploded ordnance (UXO). 'You are going to have to improvise all of your equipment for Day Two of the war,' he tells us.

The Army never has all the equipment it would like, so making do with whatever is available has always been an essential military skill. Royal Engineers have a trade as well as being combat engineers, so our bomb disposal team might include every construction craft from welders and plasterers to carpenters, bricklayers and electricians. Our welders can make the frame of the rocket wrench and so we learn how to de-ball commercial shotgun cartridges to use their explosive content to fire it.

---

* *Painting the Sand*, Kim Hughes GC, 2017, Simon & Schuster.

★

The issue of my pathetic shooting skills was always going to come back to haunt me as they have not improved since Sandhurst and the whole right-handed but left-eyed fiasco and it is during the IEDD (Improvised Explosive Device Disposal) phase at bomb disposal school that my shooting is nearly my undoing. There is a terrace of derelict houses on the camp that are fitted out with carpets and furniture to resemble normal homes. We are each allocated a house and are instructed to make and plant at least one of every type of booby trap.

I work quickly to place a pressure pad-activated device under a doorway carpet, I hide a light-activated device up the chimney, which will detonate when someone shines a torch up to search it, and I work my way round the house wiring devices and secreting them where I hope to catch out my fellow RAF students. The devices contain no actual explosive – just a sound unit that will make a deafening bang when set off – but it's unsettling enough to make you cautious.

Acting as bomb-maker I have the advantage of knowing how the bomb disposal team are likely to approach the situation, so I try to find ingenious ways to challenge them. JJ and I are determined to uphold the honour of the Army by blowing up the RAF contingent in revenge for the whole mismatched uniform debacle. Being Army, though, I'm apt to overdo things occasionally, so I haven't placed one of each kind of device; I've packed in as many booby traps as will fit into that tiny house. A mouse can't cough without setting half of them off. I'm particularly pleased with a booby trap combination in the dark kitchen pantry cupboard. I've attached a simple tripwire to the inside of the cupboard door. Very basic, but I've also included a collapsing circuit so if my fellow student cuts the tripwire it will detonate. With a couple of extra triggers so he can't bypass the wire, there is no way he can make it safe without triggering it. For extra fun I've added a pressure pad to the area where he will step back once the first device has gone off. There is a perverse pleasure in trying to catch him out. I wink at JJ as we assemble in the street outside and he grins back – the traps are set! Bring on the mice.

Once all of the devices are hidden Staff Sanderson puts our names in his beret and we draw out a name to swap houses with, clearing each of their devices as we work through the house inch by inch. It's one of the highlights of the course for me and it feels a bit like a game of treasure hunt, only with forfeits. I just notice the sleight of hand that adds JJ's name only once mine is drawn. Good to see that the Army instructors are playing along. Bob draws my house and Roger draws JJ's. They are both in the first group to suit up and make a start. JJ and I stand with Staff Sanderson to listen to the students commentating on their progress via the radio. Occasionally there is a loud bang as a device is triggered by a remote method. Roger has cleared the route to the stairs when suddenly a ripple of blasts comes from the terraced house. 'Bugger!' comes Roger's voice over the speaker.

'He found the ones on the stairs then,' giggles JJ happily. We still haven't stopped smiling when a similar blast comes from the back of my house; Bob has reached the kitchen cupboard.

'Damn it!' exclaims Bob. 'Well at least it was only one,' he says, as he steps back onto the pressure plate . . .

Time for me to suit up and start Bob's booby-trapped house. The first problem is to get in through the front door. Most of the devices and booby traps* during our training are based around the Northern Ireland situation, as that is the major threat in 1989. A popular device is an IED attached to a front door, which will detonate when anyone enters. It is quite small as the terrorists only want to kill their targets on the doorstep and not the neighbours, since that wouldn't go down too well in the close confines of the terraces of West Belfast. These days, if the police want to gain entry through a locked door, they use a metal battering ram to give the lock a wallop and in they go. We want to do the same thing, but just not while we're standing in the danger zone of the doorstep. One way to deal with this is to smash the door open remotely by kneeling about fifteen feet away and aiming a riot gun at the front door. This fires a heavy plastic rubber bullet or baton round at the lock, which has the same effect as the battering ram and forces the door open, setting off any device attached to the door while we are still at a safe distance.

If I miss the lock (highly unlikely from only fifteen feet, especially as the rubber bullet is enormous) and hit the door, then it will just make a hole and I can reload for an-other shot. To eliminate any possibility of wobble or being hit by shrapnel, the gun is mounted on a tripod for that perfect shot and a piece of string is attached to the trigger. So I only need to pull the string from a safe location.

---

* All homemade bombs are called devices.

Regrettably, but not entirely surprisingly given my appalling lack of any shooting ability, I miss the lock – I even miss the door. Instead, I hit the door frame, which being nailed to the brickwork doesn't move, but the bullet, being rubber, does. Back it comes and hits me on the edge of my right ear just under my helmet, causing excruciating pain and a purple, glow-in-the-dark cauliflower ear that gives my colleagues (and so-called friends) much merriment over the weeks it takes to heal. When I finish the course I am both surprised and delighted to be presented with the Marksmanship Prize. According to the boss: 'The self-inflicted headshot is traditionally a short-range affair but as you can claim to have shot yourself in the head from a combined distance of thirty feet, you've taken the sport to a whole new level. This is an unprecedented achievement, only likely to be repeated posthumously. Therefore, you must be an extremely talented sharpshooter and worthy of the prize.'

Understanding your weaknesses is as important as understanding your strengths.

In the week running up to the dreaded exams I go down with a horrible flu-like bug (caught from the malodorous bomb suit I reckon) and take my exams over two days instead of one. There is a mix of theory papers and practical tests. Although there have been no tests along the way, we have clearly been watched and assessed throughout. I feel as though I have been under special scrutiny as the only woman joining the regiment, but JJ is under similar pressure to perform, so maybe it's because we will be working on live bombs if we pass. The first day's exams start with the chemical written papers then a practical on the trepanner, which I pass with 100 per cent, going on to pass the IED tests with the top mark of 97 per cent. I try not to get over-confident as the big test is still to come. There are further practical assessments on the use of the rocket wrench, detectors, knots, the microphone stethoscope and locators so now it is all down to the final and arguably the most important test – the fuze immunisation practical against the clock. In a real situation there is no time limit, but for the exam there is a strict maximum time allowed, to recreate the pressure we will be under.

I enter the classroom alone and there in a cleared space is a metal cradle containing a 50kg German iron bomb with its transverse fuze. On the table is the BDO box containing all the kit I will need to immunise it. Staff Sanderson and a warrant officer stand either end of the bomb, each with a clipboard to mark my performance, and then Staff Sanderson reads me the instructions – I have twenty-five minutes to complete all the stages of fuze immunisation and I must provide a running commentary on my actions. Go!

I approach the bomb as calmly as I can and check the numbers stamped on the fuze head – it's a Type 15, an early impact fuze, so I reach for the BDO's book of fuzes which indicates exactly where on the fuze head I must drill. I check all the kit I'm going to need and lay it out in order before I make the first assault on the fuze – I feel like a surgeon choosing a scalpel to make the first incision. As I draw on the fuze with a marker pen and reach for the hand drill I glance up at the two instructors who are both writing notes – that alone is very distracting, but worse than that I notice that all the school's instructors are watching from the doorway – everyone has come to see if I can do this! They need to see that I can actually do the job, they need confirmation that I am as good as the men. I know they will tell everyone in the regiment how I perform, so I need to impress by remaining calm under pressure and getting every stage right.

I place the drill bit on the pen mark, glance at the book one more time to double check and begin to turn the handle. A bit more pressure to cut into the alloy fuze head. Must keep the bit absolutely vertical; an angled hole will fail. Slowly but steadily I drill to the correct depth and blow the metal shards away from the hole before I remove the bit. I don't want to fail because a stray fragment goes into the hole. Hole complete, I reach for the screw-threaded hollow needle and carefully screw it into the hole before making an air-tight seal around it. I talk my way through each step describing what I'm doing and why, as well as explaining all the things I'm checking for – I'm trying to sound confident but I don't want my voice to give away the pressure I feel, with everyone watching and the clock ticking.

I glance up at the clock on the wall to see how much time I have left. *Got to get a move on here, Lucy.* The short time frame is to add pressure and increase the adrenaline. They are trying to replicate the real pressure I would be under doing this on a live bomb – and it's working. Next comes the plastic tubing with a valve and a bottle of saline solution. I must attach this to the hollow needle, connect the bicycle pump to create a vacuum and then with the other hand flip the switch and drain the solution into the fuze. With the solution filling the fuze I must pressurise it all with the bicycle pump. I work quickly and methodically, taking care not to cock it up on the final stages, and then I step back. I'm done with five minutes left on the clock. The silent instructors immediately step forwards to inspect my work closely.

'Well done, Ma'am,' says Staff Sanderson, still inspecting the fuze. He stands up to look me in the eye. 'You've scored a hundred per cent in twenty minutes, congratulations!' I breathe out with a sigh of relief – I hadn't even noticed I was holding my breath.

And that was it – I'd passed the course, coming second overall. Only David scored higher in the final tally. I feel overwhelming relief that I had not let everyone including Kate (or myself) down. In less than a year I have gone from being a civilian to becoming a qualified bomb disposal officer – something I could never have imagined. The sense of achievement was greater than passing out of Sandhurst, but this time it was tinged with trepidation. I would now have to actually do this dangerous job for real. Passing a test in a classroom is one thing but could I do the job in the field?

9

It's a Minefield Out There

'Stop digging! Stop digging!' The soldier controlling the digger freezes. I peer over his shoulder to get a closer look at the grey image on the monitor in front of him. The cameras on the remote-controlled digger show what has been revealed. Part of the pipe-mine he has just uncovered is flattened and bent. I pick up the radio handset beside me and report the situation to the Operations Room. 'Number six mine located but the pipe end is badly damaged, over.'

'Continue digging until two metres of pipe are exposed then report back, out,' comes the disembodied voice from the speaker. We keep on digging as gently as we can; this is going to take time.

It's been almost eighty years since the start of the Blitz so you can be forgiven for not realising that there are still thousands of unexploded bombs around the country. One of the reasons there are still so many UXBs is the height they were dropped from. As the air defences around London intensified, any bombers that were forced to turn back would have to jettison their payload to allow them enough fuel to return to Germany. As the planes flew low over the Thames to avoid the balloon cables and heavy flak of the anti-aircraft guns, they would drop their bombs over the river and at a height too low to arm them. This happened in all bombed cities; planes hit by flak but still airborne would lose height, drop their bombs and try to escape home. Around 10 per cent of the bombs dropped over the UK did not explode.[*]

Reports made after each raid by ARP[†] staff and Fire-watchers were collated to show the high risk areas. With massive areas of London bombed in successive raids the priority was to deal with bombs found in dockyards and streets, so bombs that landed on open ground were way down the list. As a result, there are still UXBs in places like London parks. We know where many of them are, but since no one is likely to build on that land the risk of clearing them is too high. The reason they didn't go off in 1940 is the reason they won't go off now (unless someone tries to dig them up of course, so any major construction project in London is checked against the wartime records to see if a UXB is on that site). Major construction projects such as Tube extensions, the Channel Tunnel and Crossrail all involve consulting EOD officers.

It's not always building or road widening that uncovers bombs. Drought is another reason that munitions are found, as the shrinking clay pushes them to the surface. Since we mined most of the beaches and coastal strips on the east and south coasts (the UK once had nearly 2000 minefields containing up to 350,000 landmines!) where we

---

[*] http://www.bbc.com/future/story/20150922-these-nazi-bombs-are-more-dangerous-now-than-ever-before
[†] Air Raid Precautions.

thought an invasion force might land, it's hardly surprising that a severe drought causes mines to crop up between the caravans overlooking the beaches. It wasn't until 1972 that the last mined beach was reopened to the public.[*]

Back in 1941, with the high risk of imminent enemy invasion, it was decided that all UK airfields within an hour's drive of the coast would be fitted with a defensive system of underground metal pipes, laid in a criss-cross pattern about six feet under the runway and filled with explosive cartridges. At the head of each pipe was a pot to hold a detonator that was linked to all the others. The detonators were to be inserted as soon as the German invasion began and enemy troops landed on the beaches, so the system would be ready to fire the moment enemy planes tried to land. With this plan the government hoped to hamper any invasion force by denying them access to the runways and forcing them to bring all their heavy equipment and logistics in via the heavily mined and strongly defended beaches. Later in the war, some of the cartridges were removed as they had deteriorated and many more were cleared afterwards, but a number of airfields were sold or developed with the mines still underneath. The operation to clear these pipe-mines is called Operation Crabstick. Eastleigh Airport near Southampton is one such site with intact mines beneath it. Because it is destined to be expanded it is closed for a weekend while my regiment, 33 Engineer Regiment (Explosive Ordnance Disposal), moves in to clear the potentially lethal explosives. This

---

[*] Evans, Roly (2017), *The Journal of Conventional Weapons Destruction*, Vol. 21, Iss. 1, Article 9, 'World War II Coastal Minefields in the United Kingdom'.

will be my first experience of clearing live wartime explosives as a newly qualified bomb disposal officer!

The Eastleigh operation is the most complex the regiment has ever tackled and it has taken months of detailed planning by Major Mike Lauder. There are eighteen mines, each one a whopping 40ft long, buried at a slight downward angle beneath the airfield. Every mine is filled with sensitive glycerine explosive that has been made even more volatile over time by mixing with the rust on the iron casings. The risk of explosion is so high that six miles of the nearby M27 are closed, trains are diverted and fourteen homes are evacuated. We deploy to Eastleigh Airport on Friday morning and watch the last planes take off before taking over the airfield. Weirdly, at this stage I am more nervous about the press conference afterwards than the prospect of being close to so much unstable explosive.

There will be a number of EOD teams working on the operation, so we are each allocated an area to clear using large, remote-controlled Hymac diggers. My team and I will be positioned inside an 11-ton Saracen armoured personnel carrier parked a few metres behind our digger. The team consists of me as Number One, the lead bomb disposal officer, a corporal as Number Two assistant and two POMs (Plant Operator Mechanic), Royal Engineer soldiers who will operate the digger controls. The plan is to dig remotely to uncover the mine and then there will be an order to cease digging to allow the Number One from each team to go forward to check progress and the condition of the explosive. The digging will then be completed and the explosive flushed out. Sounds straightforward, I think.

As the mines had been driven down into the ground at an angle, we aim to start excavating at the shallow end and gingerly work our way deeper. This will minimise the risk of hitting the casing if the pipe is bent. The mines have all been located using metal detectors and we are fairly confident about the starting depth, so each mine is marked out with tape. All of the teams will have to stay under armoured protection during the digging phase, in case one of the mines goes off and blasts deadly shrapnel at us. If a mine does detonate, not only will there be thousands of shards of red-hot, razor-sharp shrapnel from the metal casing but there will also be a similarly deadly hail of metal from the destroyed digger directly above it, making a wide lethal area. The teams are spaced out carefully to reduce the risk of one exposed mine setting off another close by. The time constraint requires us to have a number of teams working simultaneously, so everyone on the airfield has to stay under armour whenever anyone is digging. Anyone else has to remain outside the quarter mile evacuation zone.

Nobody from the Army side has pointed out the significance of my being part of the team to the waiting gaggle of press covering the operation and I am really relieved to discover that no one else thinks it is unusual to have a woman involved. As Kate, my predecessor, had been the busy press officer, maybe they are not surprised that I am here. Perhaps if no one notices I can complete my tour in a low-key fashion without any blaze of publicity.

With all the talking done, it is time to actually do the job I have trained so carefully for. One deep breath, then I pick up my helmet and trudge across the airfield in the gathering dusk to meet my team. I'm not the slightest bit nervous, just worried that I will make some basic rookie mistake and let myself down. I wonder what the guys in my team think of working with me. Do they care that I am a woman or are they just hoping I don't cock it up? They will probably have been told that I did well on the bomb disposal course – that sort of gossip travels far and fast in the Army, so they may have high expectations. Will I meet those expectations? Disappointing my team would be the ultimate failure in my eyes. If they can't trust me to complete a planned operation, however dangerous, then how can they trust me as the call-out bomb disposal officer when we could be responding to anything? I reach my vehicle and climb onto the footplate to haul the rear door open. 'Evening all,' I say with a grin, as the three men inside look up and smile at my arrival.

The interior of the six-wheeled armoured Saracen is dark and warm despite the cool February evening outside. Four of us share the space with the bulky digger controls, a radio set, spare batteries, torches, shovels and no end of 'just in case' kit. Somewhere under the diesel-filled jerry cans are the cheese sandwiches and flasks of tea. We start with the tea, naturally, which I hand round as the others carry out the numerous radio and kit checks that mark the final preparation of any military operation. The first mines are lying under pools of light from the portable lighting towers, powered by diesel generators, which allows the POMs to use the cameras mounted on the digger arm to see where to dig. With everything set, I am handed the radio to report to the control centre and receive the order to commence the first dig.

'Hello Zero, Whisky Two Three breaking the surface now, over.' I confirm that my team has begun and I notice a brief delay before Major Lauder, in charge of the operation, responds. 'Roger that, Whisky Two Three, out.' He later reveals that when my voice came over the radio everyone looked round in surprise, as never before had a woman's voice been heard on the EOD radio network during an operation. I don't think they remembered I am female until they heard the voice. I am actually really flattered, as it means that they haven't considered my gender – I am just me, one of the team, and only when they hear a softer feminine voice come from the speaker do they grasp the new, changed situation.

The first few scoops are dug out very gingerly until the top of the pipe is revealed, then the two POMs work closely together: one studying the cameras and giving directions while the other concentrates on the controls, making the small, delicate movements that will reveal the unstable mine. Little by little, inch by inch, the 40ft pipe-bomb is exposed to the cold night air. We hold our breath a couple of times as other teams call an urgent halt – any bomb disposal officer (BDO) can stop all digging if we encounter a problem. Not all of the depths have been accurate so there are delays while a digger is repositioned and this adds to the already tense atmosphere. More hot sweet tea is drunk as we wait to restart. Never is the Army motto of 'Hurry up and wait' more fitting than on operations. Finally, the first mine is out! I call for all digging to be stopped and then wait for permission to emerge from the relative safety of the Saracen. All the tosh I'd been told about male soldiers worrying about women getting hurt fades away as my team cheerfully say 'Off you go, boss' and then get on with the important task of drinking more tea while I climb out onto the airfield to do my job.

As I make my way forwards to the long dark trench I can feel the winter chill and I notice that the clatter of the generators is deafening, even with no background noise from either road or rail. Strangely, I feel quite alone as I walk towards the pipe-mine, even though there are other people very near, so I think it is more about feeling exposed when no one else is. A curious sensation.

My torch reveals the fifty-year-old pipe-mine lying at the bottom of the narrow dark trench. It doesn't look dangerous – it's just like a rusty old pipe. My first problem is how to jump down without landing on it. I slither down at the shallow end and inspect the length of the pipe to make sure it is intact. The first few inches are hollow but there at the end of my torch beam is the blockage of deteriorating high explosive gelignite cartridges! I return to the warm safety of the Saracen to radio in my findings and am greeted with big grins and yet another mug of strong sweet tea (NATO Standard– milk and two sugars). 'We're on a break!' the POMs say cheerfully. 'The generators are running out of juice, so we need to refuel before it all goes dark,' says the POM at the digger controls.

Everyone takes advantage of the pause in operations to eat and relax but I have far more pressing concerns – the gallons of tea I have already drunk and am now seriously regretting. I consider nipping behind the wheels of the Saracen, but the airfield is awash with soldiers refuelling the blazing lighting towers around us and with cameras on every digger the only dark, private spot is back in the

trench full of explosives I have just climbed out of . . .
Well, needs must.

Back in the Saracen, we try to reposition the digger over
our second mine, but we can't line up accurately as we are
unable to see the end in the dark. This is no time to be
taking any chances so there is another halt in proceedings
while Major Lauder contacts the local B&Q hardware
store, who open up to equip us with giant glowsticks to
light the ends of the mines. Back to business with yet
more slow painstaking digging and we repeat the process
all night long.

By the first flickers of morning light my team and I have
discredited one mine (it was empty) and dug up three
others. I am frozen with the cold but my initial fears about
messing it up have been replaced with a zing of excitement
and immense satisfaction. After thirty hours of digging,
checking and manoeuvring the Hymac, the first teams are
recalled to the control tower to eat and sleep while other
teams work on flushing the mines out. I try to find a quiet
corner in which to grab forty winks but I am approached
by one of the airport staff, who kindly insists that I sleep
separately from the men. He has provided me with a
separate room 'for ladies' and I'm too exhausted to go anywhere else. There, in his office, is a small camp bed and
a sleeping bag and thirty seconds later I am sound asleep,
surrounded by the comforting and familiar airport noises.

No one I speak to that weekend makes any comment
to me about a woman doing the job, so with the lads in
my team clearly having no problem working closely with
me I wonder what all the fuss has been about. In theory it
is a major breakthrough for all women in the military but

in practice everyone realises that the task at hand is more important than the sex of anyone on the team.

My exploits while clearing the pipe-mines at Eastleigh Airport on Operation Crabstick have brought me to the attention of the national press, as the morning after the massive operation brings a page three, quarter-page article in the *Telegraph*, with the headline 'ARMY SENDS IN WOMAN TO CLEAR MINED AIRPORT', alongside a photo of me in a trench clasping a section of a mine. As if I did it all on my own! I think it is sad that a single woman doing the job is considered more newsworthy than the sheer scale of the operation. I had naively hoped to be more of an interesting footnote rather than the whole story.

The Army 'powers that be' are very happy with the photo and the coverage generally, though, so it is followed up with more requests for interviews and a photo shoot with *Woman* magazine. I am told by the MoD press desk to play the game and stick to the basic script of more opportunities for women. I'm deeply frustrated by the fact that I am currently the only female BDO and will remain the only one unless they change the restrictions, since all women still have to join the WRAC rather than the Royal Engineers and the only WRAC post is mine. My fifteen minutes of fame continues with a number of radio interviews and a *Telegraph* cartoon of two female soldiers putting on make-up and reminding each other to keep their powder dry, then a large serious article in an East Asian in-flight magazine* – a real mixture of media

---

* *Signature*, March 1991.

interest. In one interview I am asked 'What is your favourite colour?' and 'Which was the last album you bought?' so they were not exactly highbrow journalistic pieces.

No sooner has the media interest died down than we are visited by Tom King, the Secretary of State for Defence, so the TV cameras are back in my face once more. I am wheeled out yet again to illustrate how the modern Army is moving forward. The following day is the regimental Open Day where I am cast as a damsel in distress to be rescued by the lads, either by building bridges or by carrying me across obstacle courses on a stretcher or in a wheelbarrow. After feeling so buoyant during the operation and getting used to being treated just like anyone else on the team, it is dispiriting to be a novelty and be treated so differently. By the end of the day I am black and blue and feeling less than generous towards the 'modern' Army.

10

Defusing the Situation

'Ladies first,' he says.

'After you, Sir,' I say, still saluting smartly.

'No, no, my dear, after you.' He's not moving.

'Really Sir, after you,' I repeat, getting desperate now.

'My dear, I insist.'

This isn't going according to plan. As the only second lieutenant in the regiment and therefore the most junior officer, I am tasked to open the mess door for the Engineer-in-Chief to meet the other Royal Engineer officers waiting in the anteroom and then follow him in. He has come to visit the bomb disposal regiment and also talk to the officers about their career progression, but as I am WRAC and not a Royal Engineer I am on door-opening duties. He refuses to go through the open door, so we have an embarrassing five-minute standoff with neither of us willing to go through the door first. Eventually (he is getting cross) I go through the door in front of him and receive a withering look from the Colonel for both running late and entering the room first, so it looks as if everyone stands up for me and not the General. You just can't win.

My relief at having successfully passed the Advanced

Bomb Disposal Course* on 23 December 1989, less than a year after joining the Army, is cut short when Nick, the Adjutant, discovers while checking the records that I have missed a key qualification because as a woman I am not a capbadged Royal Engineer.

I believed that once I had completed a six-month period of practice I could be declared operational but all the men have completed a Demolition Safety Officer course as an integral part of their Royal Engineer training and I have missed out on this stage by going straight to the bomb course. It's imperative that I qualify quickly and quietly before anyone realises I'm not qualified on demolitions and definitely before going onto the Duty BDO Roster. The only course that is available at such short notice is a Territorial Army Young Officers' Course (initial post-Sandhurst training for Engineer officers), which includes the vital missing demolitions module.

There's always been a certain amount of friction between the two organisations despite many, like me, being ex-TA. They call us 'ARABS' or Arrogant Regular Army Bastards and we refer to them as 'STABS' or Stupid Territorial Army Bastards. Therefore I am firmly instructed that I have to maintain the honour of the Regular Army at all costs. I am ordered to be first there every morning, be the first to hold my hand up for every question, come top in every test and under no circumstances let the TA show me up. No pressure then.

During the first part of the course I learn to categorise

---

* Officers start with the advanced course while the elementary and intermediate courses are for the soldiers learning EOD equipment and related operations.

and blow up bridges according to their construction method, such as arch or suspension, and this proves to be such fun that I have never since driven under or over a bridge without mentally ticking off its category and the best method of blowing it up. Yet another habit I can't shake off.

A key part of the course is mine warfare and learning that the aim of a minefield is to control the terrain, thereby keeping the enemy in a vulnerable position. Along with the TA junior officers, all straight from their short Sandhurst course, I learn to recce* a minefield (full of practice mines) under the cover of darkness. The idea is to discover how far the minefield extends, what kind of mines are in it and how thickly they are sown, in order to decide whether to risk going around or through the danger zone. This recce involves crawling across the minefield in the dark and feeling with our bare hands for any surface-laid mines, using a short piece of wire to feel over our heads for tripwires that would activate jumping mines and prodding the ground carefully with a spike to locate buried mines. Then we crawl forwards a few inches and repeat the process. We mark the mines discovered and measure the distances between them as we crawl.

After about ten minutes of crawling and searching I'm cold, I'm soaked by the dew, I've skinned my elbows and knees on the flints in the field and I've met every thistle and stinging nettle that Kent has to offer. My bare hands are both numb and stinging at the same time. To make matters worse, I am getting left behind by the TA,

---

* Recce is reconnaissance or finding the enemy strengths.

who just aren't doing it properly. They are half crawling, half standing and giving things a bit of kick and I can see this exercise isn't going to end well for me. Within a few minutes they will reach the other side of the minefield, realise that I am so far behind and start up a slow hand clap followed by a few verses of 'Why are we waiting?' I stand to suffer no end of teasing and mickey-taking about the Regular Army being last. There are a lot of them and only one of me so I decide to fend off any criticism by showing off my new-found EOD skills. My plan is to defuse the mines as I go along and so when I am asked 'What took you so long?' I shall be able to reply 'We *professional* officers have military skills that you *amateur* ones don't,' and thus restore the balance of one-upmanship. An excellent plan. Or so I thought.

A few moments later I come across an anti-tank mine in the rough grass. It is the size of a hub-cap, with a raised fuse cap on the top. This particular type is really easy to defuse – you just unscrew the fuse cap and take the top off. I can feel the rough surface of the serrated-edged fuse cap so I try to get a grip of it with my right hand, but my fingers are so numb it is hard to get a good handhold. I try again with my left and have the same problem. Although I can clearly feel the rough circle of the fuse cap on the top, it just won't turn. I fiddle with it for a full five minutes but it is clearly too rusty, so in frustration and as time is passing I wrap one arm around the mine, grip the fuse cap with the other hand and give it an extra hard twist. I finally feel it give and at that very moment it dawns on me that it is not an anti-tank mine – it is a crusty cowpat! I am called Captain Cowpat for *years*. I never really live it down – but

I do learn the valuable lessons of never showing off in front of the TA and never trusting a man with night vision goggles as he'll be watching you and telling everyone what you're doing.

'Captain Cowpat' was actually quite a good nickname by Army standards, as I was only a second lieutenant at the time and it sounded like I'd been promoted. Much is made of the military sense of humour and banter, which plays a key part in the bond between comrades. The ability to laugh at yourself is vital to maintain a balance in a hierarchical organisation like the armed forces, where egos can overinflate with a rise in rank. Nicknames are a case in point; they are basic and usually inspired by a perceived flaw, an amusing surname or your silliest mistake. Sometimes the name is ironic, so 'Lofty' might be short of stature and 'Ten-inch' Thompson is not complimentary whereas 'Two-inch' Tennison was a legend. Corporal Kerr is predictably 'Wan' and Corporal Daley is 'Twice'. A personal favourite is Thrombo (short for thrombosis) – a slow-moving thick clot. My nickname is wearing thin by the time I am a major, but it is certainly better than a WRAC friend who was known as 'No-Tits Newman'; she was keen to get married so she could change her name but has been universally called 'Tit-less Taylor' ever since.

I remain high profile after my first bomb disposal operation. The media are still following my every move and all of the reports are supportive, but one of the more significant pieces is the *Woman* magazine double-page spread. I am one of the five women chosen to represent the nineties. The article is titled 'Women of the 90s' as we are 'remarkable people who have jobs, a passion or a cause they feel strongly about and which has inspired them to do great things'.[*] The feature covers the head of Patak Foods, an egg donor, a gardener, a badger campaigner and me – quite an eclectic mix. Unfortunately, not only do they spell my name wrong but, far worse, they give me the cringe-making strapline 'I need nerves of steel and a steady hand', which makes my heart sink as soon as I see it. I dread to think what the lads will make of that. I have already suffered more than enough with the *Telegraph* airfield photo of me holding the 5ft section of pipe-mine, which was the star picture of the regimental caption competition. Squaddie humour is legendary and rather basic in its schoolboy nature, so they are never going to let me get away with that toe-curling strapline, even though I didn't actually say it. I don't think the lovely article writers at *Woman* ever thought that line through . . .

Part of my role as the regimental press officer is to deliver general interest lectures on bomb disposal to schools and one of the first schools I visit is an all-male independent school that has a cadet force. They have booked a bomb disposal expert to come and impress the boys with talk of bravery and daring and are most unhappy that I have turned up and not a man. So sorry.

One of the regimental officers points out that as my profile has suddenly risen with all the publicity it also raises my personal risk, so I should take extra precautions with my personal security – particularly as I live 'outside the wire' or outside the protection of the barracks. Even

[*] *Woman*, 11 February 1991.

though the shared house I live in is right next to the back gate, there are no cameras covering my car and there is only one route up the hill to the regiment. To make me appreciate how my new status could be exploited by those who would wish me harm he suggests that I design a booby trap that will only kill a woman. Once I realise how easily I can be specifically targeted I will be more aware and therefore less vulnerable. After much thought about my routine and those of other women, I design a small shaped charge fitted behind the detergent drawer of a washing machine. It is armed by selecting the 'delicates' cycle and detonates as the victim bends down to start the machine. Horribly sexist but horribly effective.

In the late summer of 1990, when I am a fully-fledged bomb disposal officer, the invasion of Kuwait by Iraqi forces draws our attention away from routine bomb disposal. Instead, the regiment is fully focused on going to war to push Saddam Hussein's forces back to Iraq. The Americans call the First Gulf War 'Desert Storm' but for us it is 'Operation Granby'.

One of our squadrons, 49 EOD Squadron, will deploy to the Gulf as part of the UK's 1st Armoured Division but as past EOD operations in war have recorded a high casualty rate for Number Ones the squadron will have additional officers attached to support EOD operations, including neutralising minefields and boobytraps laid by the retreating enemy troops. I have my fingers crossed I might be one of the extra Number Ones, but any hopes I have about deploying are quickly quashed. I cannot be on the deployment list for two reasons: partly because I would be a lone woman in an all-male unit that may be remote from other units and partly because they need to leave a certain number of officers behind to cover EOD work in the UK, where security will be much tighter. Over 200 WRAC servicewomen will deploy but these are either in Headquarters or grouped in support units such as the Royal Military Police. It's particularly telling that only one of the forty female cadets who were commissioned with me is allowed to deploy to the Gulf with her unit. The WRAC agreed to let me operate in the UK, but going to war is a step too far, too soon.

I'm obviously frustrated but not really surprised; women's progress has been taken in baby steps so far and although I'm bitterly disappointed I understand their reluctance to take the big step of allowing me to deploy at this time. I will need to consolidate the female position in bomb disposal by successfully completing a full tour of EOD operations before the WRAC hierarchy can contemplate progressing to deployment in war. The prospect of the first female bomb disposal officer also being the first to lose her life in action might undermine and set back the wider employment of women in the Army if there was a media outcry. It is over twenty years later when the first female bomb disposal expert, Captain Lisa Head, is killed in Afghanistan in 2011 and in the event there is absolutely no public protest whatsoever about women doing dangerous jobs. She isn't the first woman to be killed in the war and the parade of coffins flying into Wootton Bassett is becoming a regular sight on our TV screens. The concern is over the number of troops losing their lives, regardless of their gender.

During my two-year tour of duty in bomb disposal I develop more problems with my right hand; the two outside fingers are tingling with pins and needles and going very cold and stiff, so I am referred to a specialist for tests. If my hand problems persist I will be medically downgraded, which will seriously hamper my career and promotion prospects. As I line up to salute the last Land Rover rolling out of the gate to deploy to the First Gulf War I notice that I can't feel the outer fingers on my saluting hand at all. Tests reveal that the side of my hand has started to wither and I have a lesion on my ulnar nerve, making my little finger and part of my ring finger numb. It was probably caused by being stretched over wrist bones that are in the wrong place. Whatever has caused it, the result is I am signed off as temporarily unfit for EOD duties but fit for everything else. This hits hard and I feel redundant and very low. So many of my friends have gone to war and there are no more bomb disposal duties in the foreseeable future. I didn't want my tour to end this way but I can't see a solution to the problem. Despite the best medical help my doctor father and physio mother can give me there is nothing more to be done.

One Army medic suggests that I have my numb little finger amputated as it sticks out and is constantly being injured, catching in my pistol mechanism. After I've accidentally ironed and fried the finger a few more times and then shut the car door on it and walked away, breaking it yet again, I am ordered to attend a medical board. I am surprised to notice that none of the three Army doctors has the same number of fingers they were born with. They explain their own injuries to me and the restrictions they suffer, including the difficulty of a narrow grip, before deciding that I should keep the finger and not be medically downgraded. I then strap my numb little finger to my only-slightly-tingly ring finger with a rubber band and everyone is happy. Problem solved.

With Coalition attacks and air strikes on Iraqi forces all day and all night, Operation Granby means that the security situation has escalated, so every UK base is now on a higher alert, with increased armed guards and more restrictions. In fact, all military activities are to have higher protection, as we can expect to be attacked anywhere in the world. With this in mind, it is agreed that I will accompany elements of the Parachute Regiment on exercise in Europe. The Parachute Regiment is a high-profile target for terrorists, especially the IRA, due to their deployments in the Province and so they are at increased risk now. The training is called Exercise Winter Warrior, which I quickly discover is skiing in the French Alps. Not quite the desert combat that my regiment is involved with!

As soon as the sixty-five male paratroopers and the three women (a captain, a sergeant instructor and me) arrive at the accommodation there is a briefing from the organising officers. 'Is anyone here AT trained?' asks a senior officer, referring to the Ammunition Technicians of the Royal Army Ordnance Corps – those soldiers trained to inspect, store and destroy all forms of ammunition. 'If so, I have a job for you.' He looks around the room in hope of a volunteer. I glance around the silent faces, noting that no one is trained in munitions and explosives, so I put my hand up. 'I'm a bomb disposal officer, if that's any help,' I say, wondering what the task might be. There are hushed exclamations from the young Paras and a scraping of chairs as they strain to see which of the women spoke. They look at me with a new respect.

'Wow!' says the officer, visibly shocked. 'The real thing!' he adds, as he regains his composure. 'You will be excused all other duties as we need you to search the bus every journey for terrorist bombs and devices,' he explains. With the Paras having lost a number of soldiers in previous Northern Ireland bus bombings and the possibility of a barometric bomb (one that is detonated by a change in altitude) my task is to go to the bottom of the mountain each morning to search the bus for bombs, then ride to the hotel halfway up the mountainside. The Paras will then board the bus to the top and ski all day. I am able to ski too as long as I'm back early to search the bus before the troops climb back on. Hardly an arduous job.

On the first morning, having searched every inch of the bus, I'm assigned to supervise a small group of mainly teenaged paratroopers who have never skied before and a sergeant staff car driver who is at a loose end because his senior officer has gone to war. I make sure they all have the right kit and I help demonstrate how to use the chair lift to get to the nursery slopes. I get on the lift first alongside the instructor, with the staff car driver going at the back to make sure everyone gets on safely. About halfway up the mountainside the chairs bounce around as though on a trampoline and there is considerable shouting and swearing going on behind me. When it all falls silent, I turn around to see the chairs are swinging empty apart from the lonely staff car driver. The little wotsits have jumped!

I am powerless to do anything but ride the chair lift to the first station and then stay on board to go back down to try to find them. I discover that Paras are up for anything, so when one of them dared the others to jump – off they all went. After I retrieve the group and replace some skis broken on landing, we finally arrive at the nursery slopes.

The female sergeant instructor explains the basic snow-plough. 'To go slowly or stop you need to place your skis with the tips together like this and the ends far apart at the back to make a snowplough shape.' She demonstrates the position and continues. 'To go faster you place the skis at a more parallel angle . . . ' She never finishes the sentence as the Paras put their skis tightly together, crouch over their poles, yell 'Banzai! Last one to the bottom's a wuss,' and vanish. Again. It's at this point that I realise this is going to be a very long fortnight. Eventually I get them back to the top of the slope. After I have read the Riot Act they behave themselves and very quickly learn to ski.

At the end of the first day the instructor says she will ski to the bottom and watch each of us ski down in turn so she can check our progress. I ski down first, quite slowly as I'm twenty-six and a bit worried about my knees, next comes the staff car driver who skies even slower as he is thirty-four and worried about his back and his knees and then – nothing. Not a teenaged Para in sight. We wait a while and then split up to go and look for them. When the ski instructor finds them they are daring each other to lob themselves off the ski jump. I'm convinced that this is why the vast majority of the Army is young and male – unstoppable and fearless.

It is a bizarre experience: skiing all day and then returning to the hotel to watch the war unfold on CNN. The war feels very remote yet also close to home, knowing that so many friends and colleagues are involved. It is like a party to which I have not been invited, but then neither have the Parachute Regiment. After two weeks playing in the snow, skiing, building snow shelters and learning some basic winter fieldcraft we board the bus back to the day job.

The regiment seems empty without the squadron and a number of my friends who have deployed but the hectic work schedule keeps me busy. Then one day the Adjutant says: 'Lucy, are you free? The CO wants a word.' That sounds ominous but I'm in his office moments later, standing to attention in front of the imposing desk.

'I don't know if you were aware but there is a prize called "The EOD Pot".' He waves at the silver cup sitting on his desk. 'The squadron commanders all voted for the subaltern* or captain who demonstrates the most endearing combination of professionalism, commitment, approachability, example, humour and ability to get on with others,' he says, reading the sheet of paper beside the cup, 'and that's you so do get your name engraved on it.'

I stand there silent for a moment as I'm shocked at the honour, but I quickly regain my composure. 'Thank you, Sir, that's wonderful.' I'm really flattered and touched to have my colleagues' approval. I've just been doing my job as best I can.

'Did you know about this?' I ask the Adjutant later.

---

* A subaltern is a term for a junior officer.

'Yes,' he says, 'but they wouldn't let me veto it,' he adds with a wink. 'Just spell your name right on the engraving – apparently people get upset if Stephens is spelled with a "V",' he jokes.

Although the actual ground phase of the war lasts a short time, around a hundred hours before the remnants of the invasion force flee back across the border into Iraq, the preparations and last-minute diplomacy before the first Coalition shot is fired are a very tense time for everyone, not least the families of those soldiers deployed to the Gulf. The 15 January 1991 deadline for the Iraqi forces to withdraw from Kuwait and avoid war passes without any movement, so the Allies plan to attack the following day with the most devastating air assault in history. We maintain a tense radio silence in the run-up as our squadron is in position, ready to deal with mines and booby traps left behind by retreating forces. The Commanding Officer holds a briefing session about the difficult days ahead and I nip out of the room briefly to go on an errand. On my way back to the office I hear a phone ringing and ringing in the Regimental Sergeant Major's office. I wouldn't normally have dared to answer his phone but the Headquarters is deserted and it may be important, so I step into his office and take the call.

It is the mother of one of the young soldiers deployed in the Gulf. She has just come back from work and is suddenly overwhelmed with helplessness and worry about her only son. With no one she can talk to about her fears and emotions she wants to speak with someone who understands. I have no useful or new information to give her and while I don't know her son personally I am part of his team and on his side, which is what matters. I tell her that he understands and accepts the perils of his profession and that he is not alone; he is alongside his friends, who will look after him. He trusts them to keep him safe, just as they trust him with their lives. This is what we do. We speak for an hour and I hope I helped her. She can share her worries and her feelings knowing that I will empathise in a way her civilian friends simply cannot. It makes me realise that although we, as soldiers, accept the risks we face, our families have no choice and are not as prepared as we are to handle them – but they have to cope with the risks too. Years later, mothers of soldiers serving in Afghanistan will send their sons hand-altered boxer shorts that have tapes sewn into the bottom hems, so their mates can make a tourniquet and stop them bleeding to death when their legs are blown off.

For the first time I stop and consider the worry I have already put my parents through without giving them a second thought, first disappearing off for months at sea in an old wooden ship with no communications and then running all the risks of an operational bomb disposal officer. They patched me up at Sandhurst whenever I was injured and with my father being a doctor and my mother being a physiotherapist, it meant that I could have treatment for the blisters, inflamed tendons and torn muscles over a weekend at home. My mother fitted bespoke felt pads inside my boots to mould around my swollen tendon lumps and take the pressure off tender areas. I would not have been able to continue in training had I not had urgent treatment from my family before important marches and challenges. Not once did they try to talk me out of anything or tell me of their fears. Parents put up with a lot.

I I

The Big Bang

We arrive at the neat new housing estate for this, my first
call-out. I'm conscious that we are the most exciting thing
happening right now and all the curtains are twitching in
the surrounding houses as Corporal Gregg pulls the Bomb
Disposal Land Rover up to the kerb behind the police car.
My every move will be watched by members of the public,
so I climb down a little unsteadily from the Land Rover,
take a deep breath and stride purposefully towards the
uniformed policeman waiting for me at the edge of the
cordon in front of the house.

'Afternoon!' I smile, as I get closer. The middle-aged,
bespectacled policeman returns my smile. 'What have you
found for us today?' I say brightly, hoping I don't sound as
if this is the first time I've had this conversation. Corporal
Gregg, my Number Two, has locked the Land Rover and
is deliberately standing just behind me with the camera, so
there is no mistaking who the policeman should be talking
to.

The policeman is totally unfazed by me and explains
that the homeowner has been digging in the garden and
has found what looks like a bomb – would I like to come

and take a look? I ask a couple of sensible questions to give my stomach time to settle after the churning journey. 'How big is it?' Basic first question.

'It's about four inches wide and at least six inches of it is showing above the mud, but I haven't touched it,' comes the response.

'So it hasn't been moved at all?'

'Not since the homeowner found it and he didn't lift it – just a clunk against his fork.'

I ask a couple more questions, make some notes, check the cordon arrangements to make sure no one is in range and nod to Corporal Gregg to follow me into the garden at the back of the four-bedroomed detached house. The view of the square garden is not inspiring, just the sea of bland mud familiar to all first occupiers of new homes. The policeman points to a garden fork sticking out of the mud near the back fence and I can see a trail of widely spaced footprints leading across the mire from the fork to the back door. Someone was running.

The policeman hunches down into his jacket and returns to the safety of the front door, so I take the camera offered by Corporal Gregg and walk alone towards the garden fork and the hole beside it. I'm still feeling rather cheated that my first ever call-out is just for a single munition. When I peer into the hole that was the homeowner's first forkful of earth I can see the distinctive shape of a 4-inch artillery shell lying in the muck. I squat down to look closer and can clearly see the rifling grooves on the copper band around the base of the half-buried shell. These distinctive grooves are made as the shell twists through the gun barrel and tell me that it has been fired. The nose of the shell is smooth metal and there is no fuse. I take a couple of photos before picking it up and turning it round to see that the pyrotechnic tracer[*] pocket is empty. Completely safe. I sigh and grimace with a palpable sense of anti-climax – nothing to defuse or even to blow up. I beckon Corporal Gregg over, point to the marked band and smooth nose and say nothing. He briefly looks saddened and I totally understand. We both desperately want to find a large un-exploded World War II bomb that we can call our own. Whoever is on duty when one is found gets to defuse it, even if it takes half the regiment to help.

'Not this time, Corporal G.' I realise that I'm bitterly disappointed as I had hoped for something that would truly challenge me. Despite the nerves on the journey, I really wanted this to be a bigger job, one that would put all the skills I have learned as an EOD Number One to the test. Any bomb job, whether big or small, has the potential to go wrong and cost not just the lives of the immediate team but other people too. If one small part of the procedure is missed then there may be consequences. Although the solid shot poses no danger beyond being dropped on my toe the job does not finish there.

As we pack the shell into a carrying box ready to remove it, I look around the garden. Where there is one shell, I thought, there may be more. I decide to investi-gate further. It's a brand-new house on a new estate, so how did the shell come to be buried in the topsoil of the garden? I look again at the freshly spread earth. It's topsoil

---

[*] A tracer round is one which is has a small pyrotechnic charge that allows it to be seen in flight, indicating the direction of fire.

that doesn't belong here. Sourced from a disused MoD range seems the most likely explanation. There could be hundreds of live and fired shells all over the estate. 'Get the metal detectors Corporal G, we'll check the rest of this garden and I'll update the Duty Field Officer – this may be a big job after all!'

Although the housing estate bomb is neither my first nor my largest bomb – and it definitely isn't the most dangerous of my bomb disposal career – it is still significant because for the first time a woman has been deployed to an emergency call-out as the Duty Bomb Disposal Officer: an important step for the wider acceptance of women's expanding role in the armed forces. Now that the precedent has been set it should ease the path of all women following in my footsteps. I do not just have to convince my male colleagues in the bomb disposal world but I also need to prove to the rest of the Army that women can successfully be deployed in this hitherto exclusively male sphere of military operations. I hope I can set an example too for women to be able to think and see themselves as BDOs.

One morning, near the end of my two-year tour in bomb disposal, a bombshell appears on my desk. A metaphorical one, fortunately – a letter from the WRAC explaining that it is to disband in a few months' time to allow women to be integrated alongside their male colleagues doing the same job. I already know that I can't stay with the Royal Engineers Bomb Disposal Regiment because there is only one WRAC post and I'm not eligible to become a Royal Engineer as the only role open to women at this time is that of a qualified civil engineer – so no more bombs.

The disbandment of the WRAC is just one part of a

major reorganisation of the Army that includes moving various support services into a new corps – the Adjutant General's Corps (AGC). WRAC officers like me can now transfer to other previously all-male parts of the Army and those who don't want to change careers will become part of the new AGC and train to be Regimental Administrative Officers in the new Staff and Personnel Support branch. Several services such as the Pay Corps, the Educational Corps, the Military Police and the Legal Corps, and clerks from across the Army, will be amalgamated and thrown together into this new AGC organisation, which is immediately nicknamed the 'All Girls Corps'. This is a momentous step – a big bang moment in military history. It is the integration of women into the male Army – no longer will we be separated off by different rules that prevent us from serving as equals alongside our male counterparts. It's not that all roles will be available to women; that is decades away. We still can't join the infantry, armour or many other parts of the Army but the ability to join corps such as the Royal Signals under the same conditions, promotion rules and deployment rules is a massive leap forwards on the road to gender parity.

The WRAC provided some protection for women, with rules on separate accommodation and an all-female hierarchy, but it is now also holding us back by restricting the roles we can fill. There could never be more than one female bomb disposal officer, for example, unless women could join the same capbadge* as the men. The end of the

---

* Capbadge means not only the physical badge on your hat but it is also your 'trade', the part of the Army you belong to, whose promotion rules you follow and who 'owns' you.

WRAC after forty-six years of its existence signifies the loss of all those special 'women only' rules, such as being allowed to wear a jumper in summer if we are cold (to avoid visible nipples in our white shirts), and women will have to adopt the same rules as men. It also means that there could be a situation where a servicewoman will not have access to a female senior officer to consult with over any female specific issue.

For me personally, it means that I need to transfer to another capbadge as the prospect of being in a vague new role involving pay, HR, paperwork and endless form-filling really does not appeal. I am concerned that the limited vacancies available to women within other capbadges will be quickly snapped up and I'll get left behind – a bit like being picked last for the teams in school PE lessons. When considering where to transfer to, I acknowledge that I am tired of being 'first'; it's exhausting and stressful to be so conspicuous and under such continuous scrutiny. I don't want to be one of just a handful of women in an entire corps with all that pressure, suffering from all the inevitable mistakes that even well-meaning men will make while trying to be inclusive to women after hundreds of years of male exclusivity. It's really draining having to continually prove you are good enough just to be there – feeling that only one false move, no matter how small, undermines all you have worked for. No, I want to go somewhere where they already have a history of female membership, where they have learned to appreciate and not constantly question the benefits of serving alongside women.

I am very conscious of the fact that I have been treated well in comparison to many of my Sandhurst peers.

Wearing a bomb badge on my arm protects me from misogyny to some degree, as it shows I have a military skill that the men respect and do not have themselves. A number of my friends who passed out of Sandhurst with me have experienced a far more negative attitude and have had to fight their corner much harder than I did. In short, I am tired of having to prove that women can do the job. Since I couldn't stay with EOD I had two possible options: the Intelligence Corps (I had been impressed by my first female platoon commander at Guildford) and the Royal Military Police (RMP), both of whom have had extensive experience of working alongside women since the war. Either of them will be welcoming and have a more enlightened view than other areas of the Army, who are now being forced or 'encouraged' into accepting women. The Intelligence Corps have some very interesting jobs but I find every aspect of the military police fascinating so I decide to become a Redcap, as the military police are informally known.

'They're very picky, the RMP,' says the WRAC captain in charge of postings and transfers, inferring that they won't pick me. 'It'll take months before any transfer can go through so we'll post you to Germany with the Artillery once you've finished your current tour and maybe you can move across to RMP after a year or so,' she tells me dismissively.

I really don't want to go to the Artillery in Germany but it might only be for a year, so I begin the lengthy application process. I am invited to London for an exploratory interview with an RMP major that is both extensive and thorough but seems to go well. As I get up to leave, he asks: 'Would you like to meet the Provost Marshal?'*

'Yes, of course,' I lie; as if I, a mere second lieutenant, could say anything else. I am shown into an expansive office where a curly haired man sits at a massive desk. He waves me to a leather tub chair as he finishes a phone call, then he hangs up and fixes me with a hard stare. 'So Lucy, you'd like to come and join us, would you?'

'Yes, Sir,' I reply, thinking that the less I say the better.

'Are you absolutely sure now that you've heard all about us?' he asks, pointing to the major's office I'd just left.

'Definitely,' I say, as firmly as I can. I mean it.

'Wait one,' he says, as he reaches for the phone. 'Thank you so much for dinner last night, it was lovely to see both of you,' begins the conversation. A few more social pleasantries then the Brigadier says: 'I've got one of your officers in front of me now who wants to come and join my lot. Would that be an issue?'

'Stephens. Yes, that's the one – the bomb disposal one. Going to be posted to the gunners apparently.'

I have no idea who he's talking to and I'm not sure where to look as they continue to talk about me. The Brigadier finishes the call with the promise of lunch sometime and hangs up.

'That was the Director of the WRAC,' he says. Blimey! 'She says we can have you, so congratulations, you are now RMP,' he announces. 'Don't go to the gunners but stay with 33 Engineer Regiment until we can get you on the next Provost Officer's course at the Royal Military Police

___
* The Provost Marshal of the Army – a Brigadier and head of the Royal Military Police. Pronounced 'Provoh', another term for military police.

Training Centre in three months' time,' he instructs me. And with that I was in!

I went back to the regiment in a state of shock. So much for it taking ages. The regiment were delighted that I could stay a few more months before finally saying goodbye to the bombs, but the WRAC captain was less than pleased to receive the order from the top brass as I'd upset the whole complicated posting plot by not going to Germany.

I loved the training at the Royal Military Police Training Centre, passing the Officer's Course and the investigations course with ease. My next posting and the first wearing of the scarlet beret of the Royal Military Police was to a Provost Company in Germany as the Operations Officer.

In April 1992 the WRAC is formally disbanded and servicewomen are amalgamated into the rest of the Army. My Provost Company, like many others, has a parade to issue all the women with RMP capbadges to replace their WRAC ones. It is seen as a leap forward in terms of streamlining what has been happening in the RMP for decades – women follow exactly the same career paths as the men. So we are not mourning the WRAC so much as celebrating the freedom to be full members of the Royal Military Police. As far as I can recall, the only RMP job that is not available to women at the time is the section attached to the Airborne Brigade and that is simply because they are not eligible for the required parachute training. The RMP women have very little contact with the WRAC beyond their initial training so most think it is an entirely positive step. They are now free to do as their male counterparts do without having to seek permission from some distant WRAC Headquarters. Not everyone shares this view, however, as many women lost the oversight of senior female officers, leaving them at the bottom of an entirely male hierarchy in an organisation where rank is power.

Instead of being women in a man's world we will now be sharing the space.

12

Déjà Vu

It's when we are serving overseas and have left our civilian friends behind at home that we rely more on our military mates and colleagues. I found this out the hard way on my first posting with the military police, when I was sent to Sennelager in Germany as the Operations Officer.

The NATO Officers' Mess in Sennelager is like none I have ever been in before; the accommodation is spread across several buildings with meals being served in a different building altogether. I am dismayed to find that I am the only permanent resident or 'liver-in' in my building, with other rooms occupied overnight by NATO officers passing through the 45-square-mile Sennelager training area. The other British resident officers are apparently scattered around different buildings, which makes socialising nigh on impossible. We aren't even ships passing in the night as we never pass each other at all. On my first evening I dress for dinner and trot along to the main mess building at 7 p.m. for 7.30 to meet everyone, but I am gutted to find that I am the only person booked in for dinner. I eat alone until a German officer turns up. He nods curtly at me but doesn't speak, eats fast and leaves. I feel like

Nobby No-Mates – this is not how I expected it to be.

Having spent a whole month learning military German I am disappointed not to have anyone to practise on, as I work only with British troops. In Germany, it is a traffic offence to be driving a car without all of its lights working, even in the daytime when they are switched off. They must all be functioning and it escalates to a serious traffic offence after dark. One morning I realise the bulb in one of my car headlights has blown, so being a conscientious military police officer I take it straight to the local garage and explain the problem in my very best German. The mechanic giggles, then has to leave to compose himself before returning to explain what I have actually said. Apparently I'd told him: 'The leading searchlight on my left flank has been wiped out and I need reinforcements before the next night raid.' Hardly language to help me fit in with the locals.

Living in a mess with a mainly transitory population has all the community spirit of a cheap hotel. Most people stay a couple of nights and many are neither Army nor British, so there is no 'gang' to be a part of. I am ignored by everyone from the Italian Air Force and the Swedish Navy alike. I still have no idea what the navy were doing there. With no communal space, my evenings are spent with a Pot Noodle listening to the radio, as my German is not up to following the local TV programmes and British Forces TV focuses its few hours of programming on soap operas (a week behind the UK) and football, with occasional Forces News. My boss is a major and the Second in Command is a captain. They are both married, so live outside the camp wire in married quarters and are rarely in the mess. As there are only three officers in each Provost Company, I spend my time mainly with the sergeants and staff sergeants.

Although I settle in quickly with my work colleagues, I am becoming increasingly lonely and isolated in the mess; at weekends the endless hours drag by. I don't know if I can cope with two years of being so alone in my empty dining room and accommodation. I am used to being one of twenty-one officers in the unit and now there are only three of us, with the other two living elsewhere. Mobile phones aren't yet common and aren't allowed on camp anyway, as they would be a security risk even if there was a signal. The only phone in my building is on a military network and doesn't connect to a regular phone, so even my family feels absent. I don't have a depressive bone in my body but I can feel myself sinking ever lower.

Fortunately, after five long months in this solitary confinement, which feels more like five years, I depart to lead an arduous two-month volcano-climbing expedition to South America. Having spent my twenty-eighth birthday deep in the jungle of Ecuador, in a brothel with eleven soldiers (don't ask), I return to Germany to find that I have been unexpectedly posted to another part of the country, Osnabrück. The key reason for the zero-notice move is because no one else wants the job and I wasn't around to object to working with the most unpopular boss that the RMP has to offer. I am actually thrilled, not only to be promoted to captain and be second in command of a Provost Company so quickly but also to escape the misery of Solo Sennelager.

Mess life in Osnabrück is a revelation. Called HOG

Mess (Headquarters, Osnabrück Garrison), the brick
building is a U-shaped, single storey building with two
corridors of bedrooms all full of young resident officers
from across the large garrison. Right next door, just
yards away, is the mess of an Engineer regiment, with
a couple of friendly faces from the bomb disposal mess.
Despite my new boss patting me on the head while
introducing me to the company (my face was a picture apparently), life instantly improves tenfold with new friends
around me.

One night the Engineers' Mess next door is hosting the
Brigade Commander at a special regimental dinner, so a
few members of my mess decide to raid them, donning
boiler suits and gas masks. Then, armed with powerful
water pistols, the raiding party bursts into their dining
room, soaks the diners, including the Brigade Commander,
and runs out through the kitchens. One of the raiders lifts
her gas mask as she sprays the diners and squeaks, 'It's only
us!', giggling as she flees into the night. Safely back in our
mess, the celebrating raiding party is certain they have
been rumbled but we get word the following day that the
diners all assumed that if it was a woman then it must have
been a prank by the Engineers' Wives Club. It simply
hasn't occurred to them that it might have been female
officers. Another reminder that women are still a novelty
in some parts of the Army. One day I receive a handwritten invitation to supper from the Brigadier's wife; nothing
unusual about that, but I'm really saddened to note that
she has written the dress code as 'Casual (no tie)' – even
among women we are using male terminology.

There are several barracks dotted around the Osnabrück

area and one contains the garrison cinema, which shows one film a month. While it is neither a quality film nor a new one, at least it is in English so we always go. Instead of showing trailers before the film there is a short clip of the Queen inspecting troops and we stand for the National Anthem. Officers are expected to take the names of anyone who doesn't stand. One evening I drive to the barracks gate and joke with the armed gate guard for a few minutes about the poor film selection. I then go in to watch the film. Ten minutes later he turns the gun on himself and commits suicide. He didn't leave a note and gave no clues to the other guards or his friends. I have often wondered if I should have spotted something or could have done anything to prevent it. Suicide among serving soldiers is currently lower than in the general population but among veterans it is far higher and continues to be a major concern to all of us who have served. The incident serves to remind me that although I am now enjoying life in Germany, not everyone is. Coming so soon after my escape from Sennelager I feel that once again I have been very lucky.

Despite the Army 'powers that be' modernising their view of women in the Army, it does not mean that everyone else is at the same stage. Even civilian workplaces in the 1990s are not places of inclusion or tolerance, political correctness has yet to make an impact and, in the Army, attitudes that would now be inappropriate are rife. I have a thick skin and negative comments bounce off me but occasionally something happens to make me take notice. For instance, our mess would often invite officers from other messes to drinks parties and barbeques and it is while I am

sitting at the bar at one of these functions that I am joined
by a junior officer from a neighbouring mess. 'Do you
spell your name with a B or a D?' he asks. I am somewhat
confused as neither Lucy nor Stephens has either letter.

'Er, um, neither actually,' I reply, perplexed.

He explains. 'Are you a bike or a dyke?'

As far as he is concerned all women in the Army are
either 'one or the other'. I'm dumbstruck.

I think I was stunned into silence because he said it in
my own mess so on my home turf, where I was off-guard.
He was also younger than me, so I wasn't expecting such
an attitude. Since then I have often thought of what I
should have said or done – poured a drink over him, hit
him, thrown him out or made a scene – but I don't think
I said or did anything in reaction. I was too shocked.

'We've found a bomb!' the breathless excited voice exclaims down the phone line. 'Can you come?' Of course
I can come. I quickly push aside the stacks of accounting
ledgers that dominate my office desk. I would have gladly
abandoned the piles of NAAFI* receipts for a missing bicycle, never mind a bomb. Just twenty minutes later and
with the familiar buzz of adrenaline I climb out of the
police patrol car into the baking hot July sunshine wearing boots, scarlet beret and green combat gear, thrilled to
be out of the formal court shoes, brown skirt and tie outfit
I usually wear as a captain who is second in command of
a Provost Company in Germany. I know I can't defuse

---

* Navy, Army and Air Force Institutes, a company that runs recreation
facilities and camp shops. A NAAFI break is a tea break with a snack.

anything or even blow it up as I have no access to equipment, not to mention being woefully out of date with the world of bomb disposal, but there is still that excitement of the unknown danger. I'm worried that I won't be able to remember anything useful, but the staff officer at Brigade Headquarters who phoned me clearly thought I could help in some way, so here I am. The infantry soldiers who were on a training exercise have set up a cordon out on the nearby Achmer training area so I stride across the open scrub towards the flapping tapes of the exclusion area, wondering what I will find this time.

A bare-headed major sits nonchalantly on the rear step of a green military Land Rover, chatting to one of the infantrymen at the entrance to the cordon; they both stand up as I approach. As I get closer I notice that the bare-headed officer is greying at the temples and a quick glance at his sleeve reveals the flaming cannonball badge. He is an Ammunition Technical Officer in the Royal Logistic Corps and has spent the best part of twenty years working with ammunition and all manner of things that go bang, so his experience far outweighs mine.

'Morning, Lucy,' he says, as he stretches out his hand in greeting, in answer to my salute. 'Good of you to come. I'm Mark and I've been called to a bomb found this morning by these lads during their exercise,' he said, nodding at the soldiers manning the cordon, 'but since it has fins at the back and a lug* it's definitely an air-dropped iron bomb. As that's your speciality as a sapper BDO I thought

---

* A lug is a projecting metal eyelet used to secure the bomb to the inside of the aircraft bomb bay. The number of lugs and where they are on the bomb casing are key elements in identifying unexploded bombs.

you might like to confirm the identification.' He smiles at me, knowing that I would enjoy being back among the bombs again, even if it is for my expert knowledge rather than my skill at making a device safe. 'Who actually gets to blow it up is all a little vague at the moment but if we can tell them what it is then we can leave the top brass to sort out who owns it.'

I sigh and nod in agreement. The legal and diplomatic maze of who owns what and whose responsibility it is to sort out a problem is legendary in Germany, where the NATO Status of Forces Agreement, originally set up after the wartime occupation, decrees that we have various privileges and immunities. As I now work closely with both the local German police and the Federal Police, I'm all too familiar with the red tape tangle that can be involved in Germany. I'm happy to leave the problem of the final disposal of whatever we find to someone else – they are welcome to the paperwork.

Mark deftly gathers up a tape measure, a camera, a couple of water bottles, a notepad and a pencil, stuffs them into a small haversack and hoists it over his shoulder. On his belt he carries a small multi-tool that mirrors the hefty Swiss Army knife I carry on mine – a wire stripper, pliers, a screwdriver, scissors, a magnifying glass and everything I might need short of an actual detonator is all hanging there, wherever I go. We each pick up a short, folding military spade from the back of the Land Rover and amiably set off towards the bomb together.

Mark and I duck under the fluttering mine-tape* held up with metal pickets that marks the edge of the 400-metre cordon on Achmer training area. As we walk across the now deserted scrubland he explains: 'The infantry company were on exercise and had chosen this area to dig section trenches when one of the lads came across a flat piece of metal about a couple of feet down and pretty quickly twigged that it was part of the rear fins of a large bomb.'

The rough grass and brambles peter out and the ground turns sandier – I can easily see why someone would prefer to dig a trench in this sandy soil rather than the hard-baked ground we have come across. We approach a slight dip in the ground and as I near the edge of the dip I can see what all the excitement is about. There, about three feet down in the sand, is the unmistakable shark-like outline of an unexploded iron bomb, with a single lug protruding from the surrounding sea of sand like a dorsal fin jutting out of the water and the rear fins thrusting up through the ground like a tail fin. The bomb is slightly nose down so it's hard to judge the length of it at first glance. I feel my pulse quicken as I pause to let Mark take photos from every angle of the immediate surroundings and way the bomb is lying, while I focus on assessing the bomb itself.

I try to remember the key elements of identifying an unexploded bomb and thankfully all those hours of

_____

* While the police may have coloured/patterned crime scene tape, the Army has miles of plain white plastic mine-tape. It is officially used to mark the perimeter of minefields but is actually used for every conceivable purpose, including wedding decorations.

studying lumps of rusting metal come flooding back to me. I look carefully at the tail fins that stabilise the bomb as it falls nose first towards the target; it's quite unusual to find fins still fully attached, as they break off or damage easily on impact. Some tail fins are flat like the flights of a dart, others are flat but with a ring of steel around the end of them and there are those that are square like a box-kite. These fins are square but something's not quite right. 'I think the fins are American,' I say, 'but it's odd that they haven't snapped off if the bomb landed at this angle and they definitely wouldn't still be attached if it had impacted somewhere else and had travelled here underground after deflecting off a harder ground layer.'*

Mark puts his camera down and considers what I've said. 'Yes, that is weird. It's not really deep enough either, if it landed on this soft patch. We should have a better idea of what happened once we've dug more of it out.' He puts his camera down and picks up his spade.

'Shall we?' he grins. I wave my spade in agreement and we get to work, gently digging around the bomb. Kneeling beside the steel bomb casing I break the surface of the sand with the spade then use my hands to push it away behind me. We work quietly and carefully on each side of the bomb, slowly unveiling it inch by inch.

'This is easier than I was expecting,' remarks Mark.

'Hmm,' I reply, as I too am making quick progress. We sit back on our heels for a moment, sweltering in

---

* Depending on the soil layers, bombs can travel some distance from where they hit the ground, so can be found nose upwards metres away from the entry hole.

the summer heat, and look at each other. Very strange. I sweep my hand across the steel surface on the top of the bomb to brush away the soft sand. 'Look!' We both lean forwards to peer at a scratch in the paint – a fresh scratch with no rust at all. This is definitely not right. We quickly clear the remaining sand from around the nose cone, use the water bottles to wash the sand from the casing and stand back to photograph the revealed bomb. It's quite clear what it is – it's an American 100lb general purpose bomb, so we can now pass these details on to the German KMBD* to arrange for its demolition. What is now also quite obvious is how it got here. As I suspected, it is not lying in its original position. The decades-old bomb is covered with small scratches caused by metal on metal contact, but they vary in age judging from the different amounts of rust on the bare metal. Some grooves are completely encrusted and others are just beginning to corrode at the edge of the scarred paint, but a couple look brand new.

It's obvious to us now that we are not the first to dig this bomb up – it must have been dug up many, many times over the years and has probably been dragged from its original location and reburied in this deep, soft sand pit. No wonder the soil was so easy to dig as it's been disturbed countless times before us. Soldiers on exercise would have immediately appreciated the hassle and disruption involved in reporting the bomb and, keen to get on with their carefully prepared training mission, have quietly

---

* *Kampfmittelbeseitigungdienst* – the German police bomb-disposal techni-cians. They clear over 2000 tons of munitions every year.

reburied it and carried on.* Keep calm and carry on – it's the Army way.

When I leave Germany after an enjoyable two and a half years I return to Victory College, Sandhurst to live in exactly the same tiny room I stayed in as a cadet five years earlier. Only now I am thirty and a captain on the intense promotion course known as the Junior Division of the Staff College. Victory College, which once held graduate cadets and all female cadets, has been taken over by the Staff College and all Sandhurst cadets have been moved together to New and Old Colleges – such progress. I will spend six months learning the finer points of military planning, strategy and command to prepare me for higher rank. Churchill Hall, another ugly concrete building, directly opposite Victory College, is where the 140 captains (133 male and seven female) on the course attend a number of lectures. One day, as we file into the auditorium with its massive screen at the back of the stage, we are met by a huge image of a female nipple on the screen. There are audible groans of dismay from the male captains as soon as they see it. This comes as something of a surprise to the seven women – we are not used to any reaction from men when we encounter such sexism. The response from the overwhelmingly male audience is so negative that the

---

* The same thing happens in the UK when on Friday afternoons or Saturday mornings builders working on major road projects report finding yet another World War II iron bomb. They probably dug it up on Tuesday but know full well that it takes us at least thirty-six hours to immunise the fuse and remove the bomb, so they can be back on site on Monday morning with no time lost.

young major who is lecturing has to justify his choice of background welcome slide. 'Well *I* thought it was funny!' he says defensively, looking annoyed that no one else thinks it is the slightest bit amusing. I am just impressed by the backlash from my fellow students – maybe attitudes are changing after all.

Not all Army conflict relates to gender; during the tactics phase of the course I travel to Warminster to practise combat manoeuvres with tanks, artillery, helicopters and troops. A particular highlight is time spent attacking a target with elements of an armoured brigade. The concept is that the tanks capture an objective such as a hill then the infantry come up immediately behind them and use troops to hold the seized ground. In the first attack I am in a 75-ton Challenger 2 main battle tank, which is outrageously exciting, but I spend most of the day commanding an infantry Warrior, a tracked armoured personnel carrier. Known as a combat taxi, a Warrior is armed with a 30mm cannon and a machine gun and it carries seven soldiers plus a crew of three. As the tanks are so much slower than the Warriors I spend much of the afternoon chatting with the crew of my vehicle while we wait for the attack to be completed. We can then screech across Salisbury Plain at top speed to meet them on the hill.

All is going very well and I am exhilarated by standing up in the cupola with the wind in my face while charging full pelt across the plain towards the waiting tanks. The infantry Warrior crew spot the green qualification bomb badge on the forearm of my combat jacket and we chat amiably over a brew of hot sweet tea about the expanding role of women in the Army. At the end of the day the crew say they have really enjoyed my company and are certain women will do well wherever they serve in the Army, including in their regiment if that were ever to be allowed. They even invite me back for another visit after the course has ended. Buzzing with the day's excitement and feeling the warmth of goodwill from the troops I jump down from the Warrior and pull my distinctive scarlet RMP beret from the leg pocket of my combat trousers. I put it on as I walk across to our student minibus and there is an immediate piercing howl of genuine pain from the lads behind me.

'A monkey!* A fookin' monkey! I've had vermin in me panzer!'

'Fumigate everything boys – we've been contaminated!'

They hop about throwing everything I have touched out of the back door of the Warrior. My mug is lobbed into the bin, followed at speed by the teaspoon, expressing, as only soldiers can, their immense displeasure and lifelong regret at ever having spoken to me, never mind actually giving me a cup of tea without poison in it. They were absolutely fine about having a woman on board but I don't think they are very happy to have had an RMP in their Warrior. You can't please everyone.

---

* A derogatory term for the Royal Military Police, possibly based on the red hat worn by the organ-grinder's monkey.

13

Cardboard Castles

It's two years after the reappearing American bomb and I'm jolted awake. The pulsating noise hits me first; it is painfully deafening with a repetitive low note thump. I feel it as much as hear it. It is early morning, six months after my thirtieth birthday in the spring of 1994, just outside Belfast in Northern Ireland, and it's still dark. I open my eyes wide and quickly clamp them shut against the blinding lights that strobe around the room. The walls begin to flex with the incredible pressure waves travelling across the space and my ears hurt. Both large windows are ripped open, the thin curtains stream outwards and my toiletries, neatly arranged on top of the chest of drawers, vanish, sucked out of the window. I just have time to pull the blankets up to my chin as the pressure pushes me further down into the thin mattress when suddenly, within seconds, it's gone. Darkness returns. What the fuck was that?

As I recover from the shock of this rude awakening I recognise 'that' was a helicopter, the distinctive 'wokka wokka' sound of a massive tandem-rotored Chinook to be precise. I've flown in one, at Sandhurst, but I've never had one fly a few feet above my bed. I leap out of bed, run to a window and look down to the tiny concrete yard below. By the dim orangey yellow security lights I can just make out my hairbrush in one of the many puddles. I put on a dressing gown and head outside. The corridor walls bend as I walk and the floor bounces with each step. I live on the top of a stack of Portakabins so everything shifts noisily when I move around. Caravans have thicker walls. Outside, I meet a semi-naked man with a towel draped round his hips; he has a razor and a can of shaving foam in his hands. 'Forgot to close the sodding window,' he says grumpily, as he pads back to his metal Portakabin cell.

'Does that happen often?' I call to the retreating back.

'Every pissing morning,' came the worn reply.

I retrieve my soggy toiletries and tramp back upstairs as lights are coming on all around me. No need for an alarm clock if that thing flies in every morning. It's just after 6 a.m. on Monday morning, so I may as well get up since I'm now wide awake. I start my new job as a senior captain in the post of Adjutant of the Royal Military Police, Northern Ireland Regiment at 8 o'clock sharp. I have arrived in the Province after completing the six-month command and staff course at the Junior Division of the Staff College, following the end of my role in Germany. If my tour of Northern Ireland is successful, I will eligible to be promoted to major for my next posting.

As I pull on my fire-retardant combat trousers, which are normal wear in operational theatres, I reflect that it's five years since I qualified as a bomb disposal officer and although I have left the disposal side behind me, bombs will still play a major part in my daily life here.

Just arriving at the barracks is different to anywhere else I have served. The route to the entrance is bristling with cameras tracking and monitoring all who approach the camp and the guardroom window is high, narrow and blast-proof. In front of the metal barriers is a search bay, where vehicles are closely inspected behind massive concrete blast walls and watched over by soldiers on high alert with weapons loaded and ready. I am immediately reminded of a well-defended castle with drawbridge, portcullis, gun loops and any number of unseen traps to defeat every invader. The heavy fortification and level of security is both reassuring and unnerving at the same time. It's quite unsettling to know that the guards are watching me in the crosshairs of the sights on their rifles, even if I'm a soldier too. The atmosphere all around the main entrance is tense and watchful, with an attack of some sort expected at any moment.

Inside the well-defended base the atmosphere relaxes somewhat and on the surface at least it seems like business as normal. The military support to the RUC (Royal Ulster Constabulary) is called Operation Banner; it started after the riots in 1969 and lasted almost thirty-eight years, making Northern Ireland a key operational theatre throughout my Army service. The Officers' Mess is based around a large brick building constructed in 1940 as a garrison mess, but it has expanded into lots of buildings. This is not unusual as many messes have an overflow annex but this mess has an annex, at least one appendix, an enclosure and an attachment, and then there is Cardboard City. Cardboard City is a labyrinth of wooden prefab bedrooms too flimsy to stack, so they sprawl around the edge of the complex leaning on anything solid, with connecting spurs interlocking like a giant puzzle. Here the floors dip and creak alarmingly and the walls bow towards you as you creep along the narrow passageways, trying in vain not to disturb every inhabitant. I am lucky to be housed in a metal box in the Enclosure rather than in this tinder maze.

Cardboard City offers little protection, if any, against the very real threat of the Mark 15 'barrack buster' mortar. The Mark 15 is the latest in a long line of IRA improvised mortars and is made from a propane gas cylinder filled with around 75kg of home-made high explosive. It can be fired from a tube in the back of a large van outside the barrack walls and has a maximum range of about 250 metres, so many buildings inside the castle are within range of this 'flying car bomb'. The Mark 15 is an advanced model of the mortars used to bomb Downing Street just three years earlier in 1991 and up to twelve tubes have been used to fire multiple mortars at a target. Just one month before I arrived in Northern Ireland an Army helicopter had been shot down by a Mark 15 mortar as it hovered on a helipad. The risk of a bomb detonating while I work on it has now been replaced by the ever-present risk of one flying over the wall at me at any time.

Before flying in to Aldergrove Airport, I contacted Michelle, one of the gang of friends from Germany, who is living in the same mess. 'I'll meet you as soon as you arrive to show you round and explain how this place works,' she promises. 'It is all very different from the mess life we used to know in Germany.' Michelle had brought her car over to the Province and so she drives me out to a smart country park where we walk, chat and have tea in the café before taking a quick tour of the main streets of Lisburn and heading back. Returning from our pleasant Sunday afternoon away from the base, Michelle says: 'I'll come down to collect you at 7.30 so we can go in to dinner together. On the way I'll show you where the washing machines are and all the other essentials in the main building.'

I am dressed for dinner and ready and waiting when, prompt at 7.25, there is a gentle knock on my door. I open it to reveal a smiling Michelle wearing a smart evening dress and behind her is a well-groomed, fresh-faced young man with a very short haircut. 'This is Paul, our second lieutenant,' Michelle said, waving over her shoulder at him. I think we shook hands but maybe we didn't. I remember meeting him that evening and noticing that he opened all the doors along our route, fetched the napkin from my allotted cubbyhole and poured my wine but I don't remember what, if anything, I said to him. I do, however, remember Michelle reading the lesson at our wedding in the Academy Chapel at Sandhurst two years later.

I grew up, like all my generation, being very aware of Northern Ireland and the Troubles. When someone in my Somerset village infant school went to visit London, we were all convinced they would be killed in one of the frequent bombing campaigns. As a youngster, I thought the conflict was between unionist Protestants and republican Catholics but once in the Army I learned that it is all far more complicated than a sectarian struggle for power. The centuries-long history is almost fresh. The 1690 Battle of the Boyne in which William of Orange's Protestant army defeated James II's largely Catholic troops is still commemorated with controversial Orange Order marches every year. Generations have learned this bitter history from their side of the religious as well as political divide, so each community has sought safety in particular areas. The painted kerbstones in Belfast – red, white and blue in loyalist streets and orange, white and green in republican ones – claim ownership and warn the other side to stay away. Both areas can be fatal for British troops. Protective mesh covering the traffic lights denotes the areas where the risk of conflict is highest. Outside Belfast the partisan areas are whole villages or even counties. In South Armagh there are Highway Code-style traffic signs reading 'Sniper at Work', to warn troops of the presence of a Barrett fifty calibre sniper rifle that can easily penetrate the thickest of our body armour from nearly a mile away. It is the same type of rifle that I had earlier used to shoot cluster bombs, but this rifle killed eight people the previous year in 1993.

'The first restriction,' Andy the outgoing Adjutant tells me when he briefs me on the rules as soon as I arrive at the Regimental Headquarters, 'is that you're not allowed to leave the base until you have attended a special course to teach you the skills you need to stay safe in this particular operational environment.' Oops, I broke that rule yesterday with Michelle. Once I am allowed off base I have to plan where I want to go and then check the latest messages to establish if it is 'in bounds'. A fresh list of banned or 'out of bounds' places is posted on a daily basis but a last-minute message can change everything, so the list has to be checked every single time we wish to leave the safety of our castle. A park, pub, or shop may be listed for any number of reasons: perhaps it's in a republican area or the Special Forces may have an operation nearby or too many soldiers like going there. Having chosen where I'm allowed to go I will be told the day's safe route to get there and then I must state the exact time of my return. If I'm late back an armed rescue patrol will come to search for me in case I've been ambushed or captured while outside the relative safety of the base. I will need to go to the guardroom to sign myself out along with my vehicle details, a list of who else is with me and a reason why I am making the journey.

I did none of these things yesterday. We just got in Michelle's car and off we went, without checking anything or telling anyone. However, I quickly discover that rules that ought to apply to everyone don't. As the Education Centre is a very small unit with only a handful of officers and no soldiers they have been overlooked and no one is checking on the safety rules that apply to me and the rest of my military police regiment. Michelle turns pale when I explain the procedure we should have followed and she dashes off to talk to her boss about personal safety practices.

Andy tells me that all the domestic rubbish from the base goes to the municipal waste tip in Poleglass, a republican area of West Belfast, where it is sifted. Any nuggets of information such as addresses or birthday cards are then passed on to those who watch and listen. A regular bulletin is broadcast by the opposition: 'Happy twenty-first birthday to Kevin, who as a soldier in the army of occupation in Lisburn won't live to be twenty-two if he lets his personal information go astray; yet another amateur invader.' It occurs to me that I will need to shred any waste that could identify me or anyone else. I suddenly remember that the waste bin in my room contains all the discarded envelopes from the mail that was sent ahead of my arrival. I seem to have broken so many of the rules in just the first few hours. There is a short pause in my initial briefing while Andy is called to the Brigade Headquarters to deal with an urgent problem. 'I'll explain the details later in case the same issue crops up again while you're in the chair, but could you just read through the files for half an hour or so? I won't be long,' says Andy.

I wait for him to leave the building then I rush downstairs two at a time and scurry back to my room to retrieve the incriminating evidence before the mess cleaners reach my bin. Having my name, posting or regiment plastered all over the Province would have me sent straight home in utter disgrace, so I'm relieved to find the cleaners are still working their way round the ground floor as I rescue the envelopes from my upstairs room. What else can I get wrong?

Using incorrect words is another major faux pas I discover. One of my colleagues is a local man with a family steeped in the history of the Province and he puts me straight on a few important matters. I can't talk about going home as 'going back to the UK' because Northern Ireland *is* part of the United Kingdom, despite the republicans' wish for a united Ireland – that's essentially what the last thirty years of conflict have been about. Instead, I must call it 'going to the mainland'. I also mustn't shorten names such as 'I've just been posted to Ireland' – it is always Northern Ireland and Londonderry not Derry. As members of the Armed

Forces we are banned from crossing the border into the Republic and twenty-five years later I've still never set foot in Ireland.

Almost every aspect of daily life is now subject to additional restrictions, due to the level of the threat against us from bombs to snipers. We really are surrounded. The normal phone lines, even the military ones, are insecure and the terrorist sympathisers listen in to target individuals as well as gain information on our operations. I use a special secure scrambler telephone to discuss any specific sensitive military information in secret and luckily, as an Adjutant, I have one of these in the corner of my tiny office rather than having to use the padded telephone booth in the mess. Mobile phones are banned in camp as they are too insecure and even talking to my family on a regular phone is not so straightforward. If I want to tell my parents that I will be flying home that weekend I have to use veiled speech to give them details of my travel plans, so anyone listening in can't target me by using the sensitive information. Despite explaining the need to use code to refer to the airport, the day or the time I'm travelling it generally goes like this:

Me: 'Hello, Dad, it's me.'

Dad: 'Hello, Lucy.'

Me: 'Um, would you mind not using my name on the phone, please Dad.'

Dad: 'Yes, right, hello you.'

Me: 'I'm just phoning to let you know that I can come to the lunch you've been planning.'

Dad: 'Oh yes, the one on the twenty-third.'

Me: 'Yes, but I'd rather we didn't say the date on the phone, or any timings. Anyway, I'm flying to the airport nearest you on the day in the month that is two days before the day in the month that you were born. I'm landing half an hour after your favourite evening TV programme starts, so would you be able to pick me up from the airport about twenty minutes after I land please?'

Dad: 'Of course I can, so I'll pick you up from Stansted, two days before my birthday which is the twenty-fourth so that makes it the twenty-second and your flight lands thirty minutes after the nine o'clock news has started.'

Me: 'Oh God.'

Behind the desk in my new cupboard-sized office is a large coloured military map of Northern Ireland. The colours denote safe areas, those with travel restrictions and no-go areas. I can drive a private car to any of the safe areas but will need to have an armour-plated, bullet-proof car for others, as well as be armed. Occasionally 'top cover' or a helicopter gunship flying above my vehicle will be required to provide protection. The map is covered with little flags right across the Province to show where the various personnel in our regiment of military police are stationed; some are in the comparatively safe areas while others are based inside the eight Romeo observation towers that look out over South Armagh. In 1974, Merlyn Rees the Northern Ireland Secretary declared South Armagh as 'Bandit Country' and twenty years later it is still the most dangerous area of the Province for security forces.

Being stuck in camp is unexpectedly suffocating as there is little greenery and I am surrounded by concrete walls and flimsy temporary buildings. Just because I am inside the castle walls does not mean that I am safe – far from it. I may sometimes be out of sight of the snipers but I'm never out of reach of the bombers. This is such a different feeling from having a bomb in front of me which I have mentally prepared myself to deal with. You can't keep psyched up all the time. It's the not knowing when or how anything is going to happen that is so wearing.

Every accommodation window has a defensive net curtain that is designed to billow and catch the deadly shards of flying glass when the windows are blasted inwards by a bomb or a mortar. This gives the outside view a pale hazy hue. The constant stream of helicopters landing on the sports pitch provides the background soundtrack to daily life.

I attend the required safety training, which has the desired effect of scaring everyone silly. We learn to be constantly on the alert for danger and are warned never to stop at a traffic accident as it's likely to be an ambush, nor touch anything inviting; in 2001 a fourteen-year-old Army cadet lost his hand when he picked up a booby-trapped torch near a TA barracks in London. We watch the horrific, often close-up, helicopter footage of two corporals who took a wrong turn in Belfast being dragged from their car by a baying mob before being stripped, beaten and shot dead. An experienced sergeant explains that, like the corporals, we may be carrying a hidden pistol that cannot be fired unless it is cocked first. The usual two-handed movement is very distinctive and we may be too injured to do this so he teaches us how to prepare to fire single-handedly by using the heel of a boot while kneeling to take cover, or jamming the muzzle of the pistol against the dashboard of a car while we steer with the other hand. The 'rules of engagement', or the situations when we can legally open fire, are complicated and I am concerned that in the heat of the moment I will not know if I can or cannot shoot to protect myself or my soldiers. The instructors remind us that it is better to be tried by twelve than carried by six, so if we genuinely fear for our lives we should shoot and hope to live to face the consequences. If we hesitate, it may be a coroner asking why we did not fire rather than a judge asking why we did. I defy civilians to fully appreciate the pressure soldiers are under when put to the test.

Travelling around Northern Ireland is a dangerous business, regardless of the mode of transport. The lightly armoured Snatch Land Rover used for patrolling has a hatch cut into the roof to allow a soldier to stand up in the back and provide covering fire for troops when they are out of the vehicle or under attack. A tall metal pole with a wire cutter is promptly added to the roof to prevent this soldier from being decapitated by cheesewire strung across the narrow streets. Most of my travel will be in an armour-plated, bulletproof car complete with an armed bodyguard as driver. One of the advantages of the military police providing bodyguard teams to British ambassadors in dodgy parts of the world, as well as commanders in Northern Ireland, is that my boss has access to a dedicated bodyguard and car.

Driving through risky parts of the Province requires the driver to be armed with at least two weapons – one is usually on the inside of his left ankle where the front seat passenger could reach it and the other one is in the small of his back so all passengers can reach it if he slumps forwards. The rear seat of the saloon car is designed with a ski hatch to allow skis to be carried inside the vehicle, but now we use this hatch to pass loaded rifles hidden in the boot through into the body of the car, prior to making our escape if trapped in an ambush. I soon develop an intense dislike of the bulletproof car as the windows don't open to allow fresh air to enter and the added weight of the armour-plating makes it roll on the corners, worsening my car-sickness. At least I can escape the confines of the base, though. As it's considered too distinctive I'm not allowed to bring my sports car to Northern Ireland, even if I had the thousands of pounds necessary for even third party insurance, but eventually I buy a heap of a car which is so old it is considered a modern classic. It is therefore cheap to insure if travel is restricted to 2000 miles a year. The arrival of this car gives me a limited sense of freedom, although it brings more risk as it's an easy target if identified and bombs can be hidden on almost any part of it. I'm more used to having explosives in the vehicle not under it.

Helicopters are the safest mode of transport, although they are a prized target, so most are armed with machine guns pointing out of the open doors. My regiment is regularly visited by senior officers calling in at most of our locations across the six counties, therefore I order choppers in the same way that I would normally order a cab, although with a little more paperwork and done securely on the scrambler phone.

These visits are essential, as the brigadiers or generals need to meet the officers they will later write career-influencing appraisals on. Being one of the very few female officers in the garrison means being conspicuous – a double-edged sword. Although senior officers are more likely to re-member the meeting, which is beneficial, any flaws or mistakes are also much more visible and memorable than for other officers. Just before my first annual appraisal is due, my boss engineers for me to share a helicopter with a very senior officer going to an intelligence briefing close to the Irish border, deep in bandit country. The dangers when moving around the Province are such that everyone on board has to be armed with a rifle to secure the area if we make an emergency landing somewhere and carry a sleeping bag in case it becomes too risky to attempt a return journey for some time. I am ushered to a bench seat near the front of the Wessex chopper and the senior officer takes the small bench seat directly opposite me, so that we can talk more easily above the din of the rotors in normal flight. With our backs to the fuselage, tightly strapped in, radio headsets on and kit secured to our chests we take off and head south. The senior officer speaks to his aides (there's room for up to sixteen troops in a Wessex) for most of the journey but as we come closer to our desti-nation, a highly fortified base too dangerous to access by road, he turns his attention to me. 'So, Captain Stephens, how are you enjoying being Adjutant?'

A lovely straightforward question I am fully prepared for; I reply immediately and eloquently giving details of the welcome challenges, the balance between different aspects and the problems I am overcoming, with which he will be familiar. He nods throughout my answer and I'm delighted that I have prepared a top quality, proficient response which will score highly in his eyes. Attention then turns to where I would like to be posted next and in what capacity – this is the crux of the conversation and whatever I say next will have a direct bearing on my future career. Unfortunately, we are now approaching our destination, the besieged base deep in bandit country, and the pilots go into defensive manoeuvres; the helicopter drops like a stone, taking my breath away as if on a rollercoaster, and my stomach lurches with it. The steady cruising speed and level height are firmly in the past as the helicopter skims the trees, dropping to hedge height whenever possible to avoid incoming surface-to-air missiles. The constant climb and drop is immediately reminiscent of my months at sea on *Zebu* and the oh-so-familiar nausea comes flooding back. The pilots dance the helicopter around in the sky, rolling from side to side to make it harder to hit. One moment I am suspended from my harness on the ceiling with my arms and legs dangling down, with the senior officer below me, the next I am flung on my back as he looks down from the opposite wall of the fuselage. He carries on talking and posing questions as if we were sitting quietly in his office having coffee, oblivious to the tumble dryer motions of the helicopter. I clench my teeth against the rising vomit and just nod and grunt throughout the remaining heavily one-sided conversation. It is only safe for me to speak at all when I am on the floor and gravity can help keep my breakfast down, but even so my responses are monosyllabic and stilted. I know that I am wasting the best chance to influence my career but I feel that pebble-dashing a senior-officer with beans on toast would be a far greater mistake. The helicopter makes one final sudden drop and slams into the tiny landing pad inside the base. We race to get out as the rotors spin and the chopper wheels away into the air just moments after landing, to minimise the exposure to a Mark 15 mortar while it is static and vulnerable. Silence. The nausea fades just as the senior officer is whisked away to a secure briefing room and I am left to consider the missed opportunity and the impact of failing to impress.

On my thirty-second day in Northern Ireland something very special happens: it doesn't rain. Not a drop for a whole twenty-four hours. I decide to celebrate by going shopping in Belfast with Michelle and Paul. After the whole rigmarole of checking our route and timings I sign us out in Michelle's car and we head for the shops. We are only allowed to park in secure car parks; that is, inside RUC police stations or car parks with security guards who check IDs and search the cars first. All the RUC stations have bullet holes in their gates and we will be spotted going in or out – children hang around the entrances jotting down registration numbers – so we opt for a public, guarded car park. Shopping is not the same as on the mainland as small shops and boutiques keep their front doors locked. Michelle rings the doorbell and we look into the CCTV camera before being allowed in, although often only two are let in at a time so Paul loiters outside while we shop. Bigger shops like Woolworths have a team of security guards who frisk us as we enter and then we join the queue to have our bags searched for bombs before being allowed past the foyer. It's like being back at the airport with the search tables and quiet queues. Despite these enhanced security procedures, in some ways mainland UK is stricter. I am shocked to notice that Belfast has rubbish bins in the street whereas at home all the bins have been removed from town centres after bombs placed inside them killed two children in Warrington in the previous year, 1993. I automatically calculate how big a bomb they could contain and avoid going anywhere near them, but it seems odd that this is the home of the bombers and is the most bombed city in Europe yet the public bins remain.

On our way back to the car we wait at a pedestrian crossing for the lights to change. In London, no one on the street makes eye contact with anyone else unless by accident whereas here people look from face to face as they pass. It's quite unnerving if you are not used to it. Standing on the kerb waiting for the lights I skim the faces of the crowd on the opposite kerb and immediately see a good friend from my Sandhurst platoon. We haven't met for years yet I struggle to avoid showing any flash of recognition, because if I've been identified as a member of the security forces then any connection with me is dangerous and I could compromise her safety by showing any acknowledgement. Out of the corner of my eye I notice that she has scanned my face and moved on without a flicker – she's local and knows the score, but I'm saddened not to be able to speak to her.

Occasionally it is the Army rules themselves that increase the risk. We are advised to lie down and look under our cars thoroughly before ever getting into them, but this action will compromise us if we are being watched and there are eyes everywhere. The plan I come up with is to learn a new habit. I perfect the art of getting my keys out of my handbag while dragging out a number of small items with them; small coins and a lipstick that rolls. I can then bend down beside the car and grovel around picking it all up, checking under the driver's seat and the front wheel arch for an IED as I do so. At least I know what I am looking for so I feel I have some advantage here.

One of the IRA splinter group's more lethal tactics involves planting a bomb or phoning in a bomb warning for a particular location and then planting a secondary device in the area that people will be evacuated to. In the Omagh bombing of 1998* the telephoned warning meant that members of the public were ushered away from the stated location only to be killed by a car bomb in the 'safe' area they were evacuated to. Maybe it is my previous bomb training playing on my mind or maybe it's the pressure of the ever-present threat but I feel sure that my base will be bombed at some point in the future, despite all the security, and this premonition becomes stronger with every passing week.

In 1989, just a month before I trained as a bomb disposal officer, the IRA used a time bomb to blow up the Royal Marines School of Music, killing eleven Royal Marine musicians as they ate breakfast. To my worried mind, the early morning is a particularly vulnerable time as everyone is getting up and congregating in particular areas. I recall that some of the young lads killed in that bombing had little dignity, being killed on the toilet after breakfast,

---

* The Real IRA claimed responsibility, in opposition to the IRA ceasefire and the Good Friday Agreement.

so with them in mind I am always up, fully dressed and breakfasted long before everyone else. In the event the fatal bomb attack came at rush hour in October 1996, just five months after I left the Province. A car bomb explodes at the gate and when the casualties from the first bomb are taken to the medical centre for treatment, a second car bomb detonates at the medical centre, killing one of the soldiers injured in the first bomb. Almost every Army base I've lived in has been bombed.

It is not only security forces that are at risk from the terrorists; local minor drug dealers are threatened by punishment beatings and knee-cappings, which are regularly reported on local TV but pass entirely unnoticed by the mainland media. Incidences of the brutal 'IRA six pack' in which enemies of the IRA are shot six times – two bullets to the elbows, two to the kneecaps and two to the ankles, ensuring that the victim will be virtually immobile for life – are not even mentioned outside the Province. In response to these and other incidents Belfast has a 'ring of steel' around its centre, which comprises metal gates that close the access roads, sealing off the heart of the city. The gates close every evening and all cars are forced onto a single road, where they can be searched and monitored as they enter or leave the city. Any unexpected closure of the ring of steel causes havoc with our pre-planned routes and timings, magnifying the stress tenfold.

The strictly enforced rule to be out of Belfast city centre by midnight means the film screening ending at 23.45 at weekends is full of security forces – often half of the Headquarters personnel are there. We all rush for the exit and scurry to the guarded car park as soon as the credits appear

– behaviour which clearly identifies us as security forces.

I am allocated a number of free flights home, as time out of the Province is considered essential. It gives people a break from the background pressure and allows them to appreciate some freedoms, even if it is only temporary. Flying home is like stepping through the wardrobe into Narnia. When I arrive at Stansted the terminal may be new but all my old friends and colleagues are still here. However, there are so many passengers and staff milling around that I have to scan the faces to find a familiar one. There is a momentary pause while I remind myself that it's safe to acknowledge a friend here on my way home. This becomes a new source of stress; consciously trying to switch off and let my guard down. I see a van pulling up beside me at the kerb of the drop off/pickup zone at the airport and I instinctively move away quickly, then feel a fool as the driver unloads innocent suitcases in excited holiday mode. The familiar sight of my parents' car approaching breaks the tension: I am safe. We have a normal Friday night family supper and a relaxed chat – it's such bliss to talk to them without watching my every word. I no longer have to worry about inadvertently giving information about either them or me to the listening ears. I can be honest and speak freely and I savour that freedom, one I never appreciated before.

Back in my cottage, I find the keys to my bright red sports car that is far too conspicuous ever to be allowed in Northern Ireland and I drive around the familiar narrow country roads until I have convinced myself that I am safe. I appreciate my long-standing village neighbours – I'm so lucky to have lived here for ten years surrounded by those

I know and trust. My immediate neighbours watch over my home and are suspicious of any strangers coming down the gravel track to our little secluded terrace. The weekend passes with normal everyday activities but a few of them strike deeper because of their novelty value. I don't have to queue for the washing machine, I can cook and eat whatever and whenever I like and I have the luxury of sleeping in a double bed.

The TV news is reassuringly East Anglian, with its stolen tractors and local council bin crisis rather than the stream of harsh vitriolic voices and the tales of violent miserable deaths I have become used to. Always in the back of my mind is the knowledge that I can't afford to fully relax as I need to go back, back to the watchfulness and ever-present risk of bombers, ambushes and snipers. I mustn't depressurise too much or I'll feel yet worse on my return and have an even steeper climb back up to operational level. It's a totally different pressure to that of bomb disposal; it's a slow battle of attrition, not an immediate focused threat that disappears the moment you walk away.

I spend most of Sunday preparing physically and mentally to return through the wardrobe into a different world. By the time I arrive to check in, I am mentally back in Northern Ireland. I could be sharing the flight with anyone so I avoid any of my former airport security colleagues in case they inadvertently give me away to my fellow passengers. 'Hi Lucy, how's Army life these days? Where are you posted to now?' These well-meaning comments could put me in real danger if overheard, so I keep my head down when flying back. The initial couple of hours back in the Province have extra weight as I adjust to the atmosphere and get back into harness, only slightly refreshed from my brief sojourn on another planet.

While I am serving as Adjutant in Northern Ireland, my Commanding Officer decides to hold our very first RMP cocktail party, so I help to plan the event for 2 June 1994. Unbeknownst to us this date clashes with a high-level security conference, which means only the deputies and 2ICs of the key intelligence units can attend, so this takes some of the shine off the party. Our guests have not long arrived when the news of a serious helicopter crash comes in. A Chinook helicopter carrying the key commanding officers and all the intelligence hierarchy to the conference in Scotland has crashed into the Mull of Kintyre, killing all twenty-nine on board instantly. As soon as we hear this shocking news, our thoughts are naturally with all those on board and their families. The padres are the first to leave as they rush to help the next of kin living in the Province. Within a few minutes the only guests left in the room are the senior Royal Ulster Constabulary (RUC) officers, who sit down and spend the next hour rearranging the policing structure for the Province. At the time I consider it callous to be reshuffling who commands what, but we are in shock and the RUC officers have done this before when key people have been killed. They know they must act quickly to prevent the terrorists from taking advantage of the vacuum and the inevitable turmoil. The initial thought is that it was a bomb but soon the crew are blamed for flying too low. They are later exonerated and the modified aircraft is found to be at fault.

My Commanding Officer and I attend a number of the funerals to represent the military police, with the RUC services in the mornings and the Army ones in the afternoons. It's an exhausting, harrowing time for all in the Headquarters and we're doing well to just get through the difficult days. At one of the later Army funerals a very young child reads a poem about their missing father and there isn't a dry eye in the building. The stiff upper lips and brave faces crumble into loud sobs and the loss of our colleagues really hits home. Nevertheless, the Army acts swiftly to prevent a rush of terrorist activity taking advantage of the situation and fresh personnel are quickly posted into the Headquarters as replacements. The incoming staff are shoehorned into Cardboard City as the widows and children are still in the designated married quarters. I feel for the new arrivals as they have been ripped from their settled lives and are suddenly finding themselves in Northern Ireland among the inevitable disorder caused by the sudden deaths of all the key intelligence leaders. My friends are those senior captains and junior majors who struggle to work around the clock, keeping the show on the road. Not only do they have to cope with the loss of their boss and colleagues but they also have the strain of supporting the unprepared incoming staff. We watch over them, helping wherever we can, but we cannot assist them with their immense workload as it's a 'need to know' situation. That is, they are the only ones who are allowed access to certain information. We do our best to support them personally but I feel totally impotent, unable to alleviate their pressure or make any impact on the aftermath of such a dreadful event.

As the months roll past I adjust to the new 'normal' and security precautions become second nature and just another part of the daily routine, like putting on a seat belt. It is this ease and complacency that can be so dangerous. You can easily set routines and lose your alertness to the ever-present dangers around you. It only takes one slip-up to be fatal. By the end of my two-year tour, I am tired. Not just physically tired, although the unwanted early morning wake-up calls continue, but I am jaded and rundown. I can feel some sort of burn-out brewing; my reserves are low and I am delighted that my tour cannot be extended without a break away from the claustrophobic atmosphere of grey concrete blast walls outside every window. I desperately need fresh air. I've acquired a rescue dog that was caught wandering with a stray pack on the streets of West Belfast, so she is my constant companion for the year after my fiancé is posted back to England. As an officer with my own room I am allowed to keep a dog in the mess and take her to work with me, where she snores under the desk and plays with the soldiers whenever they visit the Headquarters. My final year alone in Northern Ireland, once both Michelle and Paul were posted away, would have been miserable without the comfort and companionship that only a dog can bring.

I fly to Stansted for the final time after my two-year operational tour of duty. I've stayed for the maximum time anyone is allowed to serve in Northern Ireland – two years and not a day longer without a seriously good military reason. The strain of being in the Province and the associated restrictions means that we are not allowed to stay longer. This minimises the risk of anyone becoming careless or complacent. My parents drive me and the dog to my cottage and once through the front door I look around my tiny two-up two-down period home. I'm not searching for danger or devices; it's more like checking that all is present and correct. Finally, I breathe in deeply. I am home. Shortly after coming home from Northern Ireland I drive out of the camp gate of my new base near Salisbury Plain and after a mile or so I have to pull over to appreciate the enormity of what I have just done.

After two years of calling at the intelligence office to find out which route to take and where I was allowed to go and then signing out at the guardroom, giving details of my vehicle, which route I was taking, where I was stopping, who was with me and what time I would be back, I had just driven out of camp without telling anyone anything. The shock is almost overwhelming. I am free! No one knows where I am, I can go anywhere I like – I am stunned. My former commanding officer told me that it took him six months back home in Wales to fully decompress from the pressure of serving in Northern Ireland and now I understand what he meant. My instinct for trouble and danger are still on high alert; I remain automatically suspicious of cars in lay-bys along my route, I make sure I park where there are a number of possible exit routes and I drive defensively, but the basic freedom to come and go as I please will take a lot of getting used to.

Decades later, this feeling of lurking sudden danger has not left me. Not anywhere. I'd been told that bomb disposal officer John Phillips survived the bomb exploding on HMS *Antelope* during the 1982 Falklands war because he was standing against the ship's bulwark, though his left arm, which was protruding, was blown off. After hearing this, it became automatic for me to stand next to a solid object whenever possible, even on the concourse of King's Cross station while looking at the departure boards. In the 2017 Manchester Arena bombing most of the victims who died were standing in the open centre of the foyer, while those standing around the walls survived.

In Belgium in 1988 the IRA walk down the queue of civilian cars waiting at the lights until they find one with plates only issued to the Army. They then shoot the driver dead. He sees them coming towards him but is trapped. As a result, I instinctively avoid getting so close to the car in front in traffic that I can't pull out and get away. And when I visit a restaurant or a pub I still won't sit with my back to the door and I note the exit routes before I sit down. I wouldn't pick up a dropped torch or a dropped anything for that matter, gates stay left open and I won't move a neighbour's wheelie bin out of the way when leaving the drive. I open all parcels standing up and never sitting down (it saves getting your legs blown off) and not over a flat surface (it deflects the blast into your face).

Life-saving habits die hard.

14

Lights, Camera, Action!

A large, strong hand grips the back of my neck and thrusts me face down into the footwell of the car.

'Get down and stay down!' is the command shouted in my ear – as if I could do anything else with the shovel-like hand squashing my nose into the plush carpet. I listen to the squeal of tyres and the deafening volley of shots coming from inside my car as the driver flings the vehicle into a sharp turn, engine screaming, voices shouting. Almost immediately we crash into something solid and the rear passenger door is ripped open while more hands grab my clothing, haul me out and fling me unceremoniously into a soggy ditch beside the road. A heavy weight sits on me as gunfire crackles all around. I can hear the powerful Range Rover screech to a halt close by followed by salvos of automatic fire and yet more shouting.

Occasionally, after leaving the Army, since serving soldiers aren't allowed to talk to the media, I'm asked to comment in the press about an aspect of bomb disposal. The *Telegraph* contacts me asking if I will follow up my earlier interview by watching a preview of the finale of the BBC's

Bodyguard series. My views on the suicide vest situation, which formed the key dramatic element, will be published the morning after the programme is broadcast. I happily agree to watch the preview as I have been hooked on the series along with most of the British viewing public. A couple of hours later I have written the critique for the article. Hollywood bombs always have helpful clocks that tell you how long you have to defuse them as well as some lovely shiny screws to show you where to start. In reality, there won't be something as simple as just a clock, there is likely to be more than one way of detonating the bomb and no operator would go for the screws, which look like a come-on – 'Touch me, I dare you'. On this occasion I quite enjoy the 'not-very-accurate-but-better-than-most' bomb disposal portrayal but it is the earlier car ambush scenes that I object to.

Watching those *Bodyguard* action scenes took me straight back to Northern Ireland where I naively volunteer to act as the Principal in a training exercise for the military police Close Protection Team, jumping at the chance for some excitement. The exercise takes the form of a car journey from A to B, during which the vehicle I am travelling in will be ambushed by terrorists. The team of bodyguards and the back-up car can then go through their procedures for getting me out of danger and to a place of safety. I should have had doubts when I was given some yellow earplugs but I've seen this done countless times in films and on TV so I think it will be really thrilling to actually take part in it. I climb into the back of a smart, expensive-looking saloon car with a specialist driver and two close protection corporals; the back-up Range Rover, containing a full team of four, is ready to follow us along the road. We set off gently with me directly behind the front passenger. A dark van approaches quickly from a side turning and blocks the road ahead, men in balaclavas leap out and start shooting at us and that is the last thing I see clearly.

'RUN!' yells a voice in my ear and I am yanked to my feet by the scruff of my neck out of the soggy ditch then quickly dragged away in the direction of some trees. 'GO, GO, GO!' bellows the voice again, hands thrusting me forwards, bouncing me across the uneven ground; I run for my life, lungs burning and with legs of jelly. 'DOWN!' comes the command as I am tripped and flung headlong into a gorse bush, while there are more spurts of gunfire. 'UP!' orders the voice, but I have already been hauled to my feet and shoved onwards, my feet barely touching the ground as we go. I hear another engine and I am then abruptly lifted by my collar and waistband and hurled onto the back seat of a vehicle and sat upon, while we roar away from the fading sounds of gunfire. The car eventually comes to a halt and I can finally catch my breath and crawl unsteadily out.

'Well done everyone, that went very smoothly,' says John, the powerfully built captain in charge of 177 (Close Protection) Platoon. 'So Lucy, how was that?' he asks me. I am still straightening my soaked, trashed, buttonless jacket and trying to surreptitiously deal with the wedgie I have gained along the way.

'Um, do they always handle the Principal like that?' I ask, nursing the worst of my weeping scratches and numerous emerging bruises and wondering where my favourite moon-phase watch has gone.

'Ah, no. You noticed then. They were really gentle with you because you're the captain in charge of their next posting, so you got the kid glove treatment.'

I now shout at the telly during inaccurate bodyguard scenes as well as inaccurate bomb disposal ones.

15

Do I Stay or Do I Go?

During my final months in Northern Ireland I am asked
what sort of job I would prefer to do next; I could command
my own company or become a staff officer in a Headquarters somewhere. Now that I am engaged to be married,
there is also an opportunity to prioritise being with my
new husband over a career move. I am well aware that
while the Army will try to post us together after our wedding it may not always be possible and it is quite common
for one spouse to take a backseat career-wise in order to
follow their spouse around, taking jobs in the right places
rather than the right jobs. Some couples take it in turns to
move to the right job or agree to spend a couple of years
living apart to take that next step. I opt to take any job
that would enable Paul and I to be together for at least the
first year of our marriage; commanding a company will
have to wait. Paul left Northern Ireland a year before me
and is a language student at an Army training centre in
Beaconsfield, so I am posted as a staff officer in the rank of
major to the Headquarters of the Royal Military Police in
Upavon, Wiltshire, seventy-five miles away. At least it is
in the same country but we still cannot live together.

I am now thirty-four and have been married for two years but I have never actually lived with my husband and am not likely to for the next six years at least, while he is destined to serve in Germany and I in the UK. I never imagined that the decision to leave the Army would be such an easy, clear-cut one in the end – family or career. In the late nineties it was a simple choice. A female colonel is livid when she learns that I have resigned and she accuses me of letting the side down when we next meet.

'Why are you leaving?' she demands. 'I've fought so hard for women like you to stay once they have children,' she argues. 'I need senior women to show everyone that you can balance a family with military life.'

I stand up to her. 'You have fought for women like me to have the choice and I am exercising that choice. I'm not letting anybody down but doing the right thing for me – I need to leave in order to conceive and if I do then I want to stay with my child.'

In the event, our departure from the Army is quite straightforward as we have an established home to return to. We have to give twelve months' notice to leave and I've been fortunate to conceive during that period. I am six months pregnant by the time we finally become civilians once again. Despite going back home to the same village, I find the reverse process of leaving the Army is every bit as confusing as joining it. I'd embraced the military lifestyle fully and on leaving it I need to be reintroduced gently to the world outside. I find the civilian universe both suffo-cating and confusing. On paper, the civilian approach jars with overly flowery language and a habit of using twenty words when two would be clearer. I despair at reading long letters that imply they are important but don't tell me what they are about. I am used to a short, factual 'this is the problem' paragraph followed by a 'these are the options' paragraph, ending with a clear request or a 'you now need to . . .' instruction. No waffle, no sensational language, no exclamation marks and all very logical. The hospital letters summoning me to an antenatal appointment are brief but with not enough information, just a time and a date, with a clinic number and 'parking is available'. No reason for the summons is given, I have no idea what to expect, there is no kit list telling me what to bring with me, no map showing me how far to waddle and no indication of how long it all might take. Hopelessly civilian.

I am used to a general sense of urgency or 'getting on with it' that is totally absent in my new environment, so it takes ages to get anything done. There is rarely a single person who can actually make a decision – it is all done by committee and glacially slow consultation. Taking minutes of military meetings is easy as no one insists their comments are written verbatim; they are basically a record of decisions. Parochial Church Council minutes in my village are completely the opposite – all nuanced comment and absolutely no decisions. After almost ten years of living in an organised environment I am shocked by how cavalier the civvy world is. People say one thing and do another: 'I'll be with you for ten' doesn't really mean arrival at five to ten – it means any time before lunch, maybe. I realise that uniforms are useful – you know someone's qualifications, ability and experience just by their cap badge, rank and insignia. A chaps' scruffy overalls and battered toolbox tell me nothing about his capability, skills or experience.

People promise the earth but deliver squat. I am used to a 'can-do' attitude where the military goes on to make it work even if the problem is worse than expected; in my new world they just shrug and say 'Oh, well' before leaving, never to be seen again.

In the civilian world, if something is done by 'Gillian' it means that if 'Gillian' isn't there it simply can't happen. This is all very frustrating for me, as I am used to having someone who is able and willing to step up to get the job done. In a military combat environment any junior officer can find themselves commanding an entire regiment by the end of a bad afternoon. For example, after D-Day, the Sherwood Rangers Yeomanry lost three commanding officers in five days. Everyone is prepared for all events and expects to have to do more than just their own job. It doesn't all stop just because someone isn't there. The sense of a shared purpose is hard to find outside the emergency services, the NHS or teaching as each faction seems to have a slightly different agenda. Commercial organisations are quick to sign you up but then lose all interest – another civilian trait.

On the flipside, without the rank system it is all fairer – everyone is messed about rather than only a few. There are no rows of comfy seats at the front for officers. Everyone is responsible for their own arrangements – it is more time consuming but it allows for personal choice. The civilian world is definitely more sensitive to the human condition. I once attended a military meeting on suicide (officially called 'Intentional Self-Inflicted Death' or ISID) preven- tion and a senior officer turned up clutching a file that had 'NUTTERS' on the spine in thick, inch-high black lettering – no one commented. Fortunately, that would simply not happen today when mental health is taken seriously by the military and is firmly on the syllabus for all.

What I do enjoy, however, is the stability in the civilian world. If someone is competent at their job they can stay in post for years and actually continue to be competent, without the pressure to be promoted and move on beyond their ability – providing 'Gillian' is at work everything works smoothly. The military system that requires support troops* to be posted every couple of years means a stream of fresh ideas and no one defending their empire, as they aren't around long enough to build one. The downside is we are constantly reinventing the wheel as no one is still around to remember that it didn't work the last time we tried it. There are flaws in this trickle posting cycle: everyone spends the first six months getting to grips with the new job, so mistakes are made or things overlooked; the next year to eighteen months are spent being fruitful and conscientious; and the final six months are spent thinking about and preparing for the new job, which means winding down on this one. Anything major is delayed until the new bod is in post as they will have the enthusiasm (if not the knowledge) to see it through. Being new in post makes you vulnerable to being manipulated by those who use your ignorance to their advantage, so even though you soon catch on to them you are inevitably a step behind. Those in their final six months are happy to sign up to anything, knowing that it won't be them who has to deliver

---

* Infantry and armoured regiments are posted as a whole unit rather than as individual people, so everyone moves location together. Corps such as military police move as individual postings – trickle postings.

it or be around to face the consequences. The golden rule on arrival in a new post is to blame your predecessor for everything, so you have nothing to lose by agreeing to the latest wizard wheeze in your last six months.

Now that I am an unemployed civilian, albeit a heavily pregnant one, I sign on at the Job Centre. The official interview is brief – 'What sort of work have you done before?'

'Bomb disposal.'

Once upon a time, middle-aged women were invisible and now they seem invincible. Women in their fifties used to be undervalued and overlooked; now they are the Commissioner of the London Fire Brigade, the Commissioner of the Metropolitan Police, Black Rod, bishops and Masters of Cambridge Colleges, all of which were just pipe dreams when these women started their careers, fighting for the same opportunities as their male counterparts.

My mother, born in the 1930s and growing up in wartime, had no choice about key elements of her life but no pressure either; my daughter, born into the iPhone generation after 2000, has limitless choices but is under too much pressure to make the most of them. I have been a member of that generation in the middle, growing up without the pressure of my every move being permanently recorded and scrutinised but also being around just as previously denied opportunities for women began to open up. However, we have still had to seize the slimmest of chances and fight to break down the barriers that faced us.

Every early step into any male-dominated environment has had to be successful to avoid that tiny window of opportunity from slamming shut again. If I had not passed the bomb disposal course convincingly and then followed it up with a very successful operational tour, the chance of more women following me into bomb disposal would have evaporated. It could so easily have been another thirty years before the chance came again, with the opening of all Army roles to women. From Sandhurst onwards I was under pressure to perform at the highest level to ensure that women could establish their role within the military. We female cadets felt the strain of not letting the side down from day one; we were all in this together. Never was it truer that women had to be twice as good as men to be considered half as competent. This pressure intensified once I began training in bomb disposal, with the stakes being high in more ways than one.

When I was at Sandhurst I didn't want to join the infantry and a significant part of the reason why is because I am from a generation who grew up against a background of restricted roles for women in virtually every sphere of life. At school, boys did practical metalwork and girls studied home economics, learning how to feed a family on a budget. We played different sports and were kept apart for most activities, such as Brownies and Cubs. We played with gender-specific toys, wore very different clothes and had an unrelenting diet of gender stereotypes on the limited TV channels. That environment leaves its trace on our outlook and expectations, all adding to our barriers. Today's young women have grown up with girl power and have greater expectations; they are not held back by the implication that they can't achieve simply because they are women. The wider environment though is often, as at Sandhurst, organised by men for men. Girls are outperforming boys at school and even male-dominated professions such as the law now have more female practising solicitors than male.[*] Even so, the law remains one of the least family-friendly professions, with few women in the upper echelons.

In 2017, when it is announced that the final restriction on women in combat roles is to be removed, I ask my nineteen-year-old son, as a former Army cadet with the Royal Anglian Regiment, if he thinks women should serve in the infantry. He is astounded that they are not already serving. He cannot believe there is still a rule which says women cannot do something just because they are women. He believed that sort of blatant discrimination ended in the sixties, as it's not something he has ever come across. So whenever I see a grey-haired retired colonel on TV spouting forth about combat effectiveness being eroded by women I remind myself that they are products of a different era and do not speak for the young soldiers serving now.

The last thirty years have been like pushing a boulder uphill, every step has been a mammoth effort, but even when we finally have equal job opportunities in the military there is still a long way to push. According to the World Economic Forum report in 2016 it will take another 170 years for us to achieve gender equality at current rates.[†] Although more women are working than ever before they are often paid less than men. The gender pay gap and its

---

[*] https://www.lawsociety.org.uk/news/press-releases/largest-ever-survey-on-gender-equality-in-legal-profession, 8 Mar 2018.
[†] World Economic Forum, *Global Gender Gap Report 2016*.

ramifications for pensions will be a future challenge. Even the government's recent plans to widen auto-enrolment in company pension schemes miss almost all part-time workers who earn less than £10,000 a year – predominantly women. For those who seek to run their own business, the number of female-founded start-ups has doubled over the last decade but there are still barriers to be overcome: only 48 per cent of female-founded companies have access to outside funding compared to 70 per cent of male-led enterprises.[*]

It's not all about money; the struggle to juggle, to 'have it all', weighs heavily on women. As someone once wrote, we have been given permission to have our fathers' jobs but have kept our mothers' responsibilities. Despite the backward step for women thrust upon us by COVID-19, forcing so many out of the workplace and back to the kitchen sink and home schooling, maybe the aftershocks of the pandemic will shorten the race for genuine equality in the longer term as past priorities and established assumptions, especially around flexible working, have been shown to be misjudged. Women's capabilities have always been misjudged.

In the military, 2020 was the year that all roles[†] in the Armed Forces opened to women, including wearing a bearskin in the Household Division and serving in SAS Sabre Squadrons. Unlike when I joined in 1989, women can now continue to serve once they have children and can provide stability for their families. When I was a cadet

---

[*] EY research, June 2018.

[†] Except that of the Catholic padre but let's not go into that now . . .

at Sandhurst, women were only just beginning to light the fuse; they were barely on the threshold of being allowed to move on from solely administrative, support or nursing roles and reach out, taking on a fuller role in the armed forces. We had to fight hard to be accepted against considerable resistance. That struggle is finally coming to fruition as those early pioneers have risen to the top. In 2019, the Royal Air Force gained the first female three-star commander, an air marshal, and the Royal Military Police have their first but not their last female provost marshal, Brigadier Viv Buck, one of my peers.

I feel that women's progress resembles a relay race: seizing the baton and running the best race you can before handing it on to the next person to carry it further. Returning to Sandhurst thirty years to the day after I was commissioned I'm privileged to shake the hand of the young cadet who, being commissioned into the Rifles, will be the first woman to have an entirely infantry military career. I feel an almost physical baton change. She has only ever known training equality alongside male comrades. Days earlier, the first woman, Major Fran Mary, passed the infantry officer's Platoon Commander's Battle Course at the age of thirty-seven, proving that women have the physical strength as well as the mental resilience to make the grade. The Sandhurst I see today demonstrates that women are now an integral part of the Academy rather than the afterthought that we were in 1989. Sandhurst's top cadet prize is the Sword of Honour, but in 1989 women were not eligible as they did not carry swords or compete on the same terms – the best female cadet wore a Sash of Honour. Ten years later a female cadet won the

Sword for the first time but in April 2020 not only was it won by a woman but she was also joining the Household Cavalry – that bastion of the male military establishment – something else firmly denied us in 1989. As an illustration of the new status of women at Sandhurst, in the Academy Chapel they sing an adaptation of 'Men of Harlech' with a chorus of 'Lives laid down for one another, all one comp'ny sisters, brothers'. This is the fruition of all the challenges women faced, the result of overcoming the barriers put before us.

The Army is not a job or a career but an entire way of life and not every aspect has caught up with the new employment landscape. The long-standing assumption, even within the Army, that all soldiers are male is still disappointingly the norm despite women comprising 24.4 per cent of the Royal Military Police[*] and 9.3 per cent of the Army overall.[†] Women in the military are in the minority and are often implicitly excluded from social events as they are neither invited to the 'lads only' activities nor to wives' social circles. Despite the advances at Sandhurst we don't fit neatly into a box. The problems with equipment remain – there is still no body armour designed to fit a woman's frame but the armour plates designed for flat-bodied men are inserted into smaller vests. The struggle for genuine equality is far from over but we are in this together and there is no stopping this particular fuse once it is alight.

*

[*] As at 31 December 2018, RMP Regtl Sec.

[†] National Statistics, *UK Armed Forces Biannual Diversity Statistics*, 1 April 2018.

I'm always asked whether there's one memory that sticks out about my time in bomb disposal and I think back to being crouched on the ground while holding the detonator carefully, acutely aware that any knock will blow my fingers off. As I'm right-handed I hold the innocuous-looking slim metal tube between the fingers of my left hand like a cigarette. This keeps the heat-sensitive tip away from the warmth of my hand and if it detonates I will still have my dominant hand intact. It also allows me to use my more dexterous hand to do the tricky bit; inserting the safety fuse into the open end of the detonator that is close to my palm, checking that it goes right to the end – if there's any gap it may misfire. Once the fuse is in position I take the crimping tool in my right hand and neatly crimp the metal edge tightly around the fuse, holding it securely in place.

It's Friday afternoon, I'm the Duty Bomb Disposal Officer for the Royal Engineer Regiment and I'm out on the demolitions range. My Number Two, Corporal Thorpe, has handed me the kit I will need: a reel of safety fuse cut to exactly the right length to give me time to get behind cover after I light it, a lump of white military PE4 plastic explosive and a detonator box padded inside to protect the delicate deadly contents. I've walked away from the safety of the blast wall towards the rusty mortar some distance away. In my pocket is my crimping tool and a box of special fusee matches that burn at a very high temperature with a barely visible flame. This is the third time I've walked across the open ground today. Every Friday it's the task of the Duty BDO to clear the UXO bunker of all unexploded mortars, grenades and other ordnance that may have been found that week and placed in the concrete blast bunker for safekeeping until demolition day.

When I reach the mortar I put down the kit and begin to assemble the elements that will enable me to make a small bomb that I will place next to the mortar. The explosion from my bomb will detonate and destroy the device a few millimetres away. I've already prepared a detonator-shaped hole in the plastic explosive; the explosive is old so that the texture is like dried-up marzipan rather than the softer Play-Doh texture of the fresh stuff. We have a stock of older PE4 and for this task it doesn't matter how hard or dry it is, so I'm getting rid of some now. With the detonator firmly attached to the fuse I place it in the lump of plastic explosive and mould it round slightly. Now that the lump and its fuse are lying close to the mortar, I light a fusee match and touch the end of the fuse, waiting briefly to check that the fuse is burning correctly before walking steadily back towards Corporal Thorpe and safe cover. I raise my arm and smile to show that I have lit the fuse and it's burning well.

Epilogue: What Happened Next . . .

Four women walk slowly into a building and into history. It is 7 April 2018 and for the first time in the University of Cambridge's 809-year chronicle there is an all-female procession into the Senate-House for the conferment of degrees. It may be a short distance to walk but it has been a long time coming.

I was appointed University Marshal on 2 April 2018 at the age of fifty-four, the first woman to hold the post since it was established on 7 December 1620. At the beginning of every graduation ceremony, or Congregation of the Regent House, there is a formal procession of four university officials from the colonnade of The Old Schools into the packed Senate-House just a few metres away; the Junior Esquire Bedell* takes the lead with the Senior Esquire Bedell following, both carrying heavy silver maces, then comes the Vice-Chancellor or their deputy in a full length scarlet and ermine cope and finally there is the University Marshal, also bearing a 400-year-old mace.

---

* One of two university officials with ceremonial duties, including mace bearing.

The procession is a dignified piece of pageantry that has been repeated for centuries and, apart from the Vice-Chancellor or their deputy, was entirely male until 2003, with the arrival of a female Senior Esquire Bedell. Now, while the cameras roll and the crowd gathers at the edge of the lawn, the four of us women form up under the colonnade of The Old Schools, one of the oldest parts of this prestigious university. We share a few words to acknowledge the significance of the moment, take a deep breath and set off on the stroke of eleven o'clock for the short walk to the Senate-House to begin the graduation ceremony. Four women launch a ceremony to confer degrees at an ancient university only fully open to women in 1948.

Led by the Marshal and stemming from 1825, the University Constabulary at Cambridge is among the oldest constabularies in the world. Traditionally called bulldogs, the Constables once patrolled the city in pairs ensuring that students wore their gowns and obeyed the curfew. The ideal pairing of Constables was one 'strong of arm' and one 'fleet of foot' but luckily today's Constable is required to be approachable and welcoming as our primarily ceremonial role is assisting guests at the monthly graduations, along with other tasks such as supporting the Proctors in protecting freedom of speech.

Cambridge graduations are a formal, white-tie affair with no music, no microphones, no clapping, no speeches, no photography and all in Latin – uniquely Cambridge, brilliant yet slightly bonkers. The entire ceremony is a magical piece of theatre, all but silent with only names and Latin spoken. For Cambridge students it is a tangible link with all those who have been before, whether their icons are naturalist Charles Darwin, mathematician Alan Turing, poet Lord Byron, climber George Mallory or comedian Sue Perkins, they have all taken part in the same ceremony in the same place. Each session follows the last with the waiting queue of guests poised to enter as soon as the final guest for the previous session has left the building. The Constables are able to smoothly empty and fill the impressive Senate-House with over 500 proud people in a few short minutes, they are so well practised at their craft. The banter and camaraderie among the Constables is very reminiscent of the Army; a number of us have a military background and we gently tease each other in the old familiar way.

I've even been in the firing line as a University Constable at Cambridge, although the missiles were eggs not bombs or bullets. For years, Oxford undergraduates have had a tradition of 'trashing' where they celebrate the end of exams by spraying each other with alcohol, flour, confetti and foam. Not to be outdone, Cambridge students have, in recent years, emulated this with what Cambridge calls 'exuberance'. While it is usually confined to spraying cheap sparkling wine over each other, the Proctors[*] and the Constabulary sometimes attend the more public venues to promote student safety and to try to prevent members of the public getting unwillingly involved. A

---

[*] University officer with duties relating to good order, scrutiny and protecting freedom of speech.

national newspaper photographer is normally on hand to document an exasperated-looking Proctor or a slightly damp, unimpressed Constable. A photograph of Oxbridge students celebrating is as much a sign of summer as an article on the exorbitant price of strawberries at Wimbledon.

One year, as a Constable, I am paired with a very approachable female Proctor and together we walk around each of the small groups of students poised to ambush their friends outside an examination hall, mediating a truce on food throwing. We have a very quiet afternoon and I suffer only a splash of cava. The final session of the day is somewhat different. Outside the Guildhall, I join a second Proctor and Fred, one of the older Constables. Though now retired for many years, he has spent much of his life as a college porter. 'Are you still dry?' I ask him, pointing to my damp trouser hems.

'Ooh yes, my dear,' replies Fred, tucking his fob watch into a waistcoat pocket as he pushes back his topper. 'These lovely young people have been ever so kind; I just keep out of the way and let them get on with it, they don't bother me.' Turning the corner outside the examination venue, we are greeted by a sizeable crowd of fully loaded students. We try our best to encourage them to put aside their eggs, flour, trifle, glitter, tomatoes, confetti and baked bean/mayonnaise combos but to no avail. It's a recipe for disaster. A moment later the first candidate emerges and they are deluged with cheap cava as they run into the waiting crowd. My military training kicks in and I react quickly to sidestep what is clearly going to be a maelstrom of missiles, so I escape all but a light sprinkling of cava. Fred, in his mid-seventies, isn't as fast on his feet as he once was and he disappears into the fog of flung flour in the throng. Ten minutes later, I retrieve a sheepish Fred from the now abandoned battlefield. He didn't escape a single thing and is caked from head to toe; flour, eggs and trifle adorn every inch of his tailcoat, trousers and once immaculate polished shoes. Purple, sparkly glitter overflows the rim of his top hat as he squelches across to the office for a restorative cup of tea, leaving a trail of floury footprints with a glitter topping. 'Bloody students,' he remarks wryly.

Being the first female Marshal in 2018 feels very different to being the first female bomb disposal operator back in 1989. I sense that I am the last piece of the jigsaw, no longer one of the first pieces out of the box. Those around me are willing me to succeed, not waiting for me to fail.

Experiences with soldiers have certainly helped in my dealings with students at Cambridge. I've traded the dark green beret of the WRAC and the scarlet one of the Royal Military Police for an 1879 silk top hat. I once wore a bomb badge to indicate my role but I now wear a gown of office – something only worn by the Chancellor and the Marshal. Where I once led a troop of twenty-six sappers, I now lead a Constabulary of twenty-six Constables; green combat uniforms have been replaced by black top hats and tail coats. Unlike my all-male troop, though, there is a growing number of women among the Constables. Women are well represented in some areas of life at Cambridge; the Heads of Colleges have an even male/female divide but look a little closer and you will find that just two of the thirty-one College Head Porters, who are so influential in university life, are female. Just like in the

Army there still is a long way to go for gender parity.

All of my experiences have led to my current role as Marshal. I've been through a number of traumatic encounters that I would have been better off without, including being caught in the crossfire of a fatal terrorist attack in the Middle East, but I believe that no experience is ever entirely wasted: they all shape your character and make you the person you are. Student demonstrations, sit-ins and all manner of protests are an important part of life at Cambridge and I use every one of the skills the Army has taught me to help mediate freedom of speech for all. The safety of others, whether they are a small bomb disposal team, thousands of proud parents or scores of placard-waving students, has always been my priority. I still have to consider the risk of bombs and terrorist actions and well-established life-saving habits such as standing beside solid objects remain.

The legacy of my military training has carried forward to my current role and who knows where it will take me. Whatever the next challenge brings – I'm ready for it.

Afterword: What Does the Army Do All Day?

Back in the late 1980s, when I first told Sue, my colleague in airport security, that I was going to join the Army, she asked me a very reasonable question: 'What does the Army do all day?'

She didn't mean the mechanics, clerks or medics, but what about the other third of the Army who have no civilian counterpart? At the time, I replied rather pathetically: 'I don't know.' I do now. Soldiers put duty before self and are prepared to risk their lives for someone else because a politician says so. With a strong instinct for self-preservation this does not come naturally. Soldiers are akin to professional athletes or sports stars who, although they publicly perform occasionally, spend hours practising set pieces, keeping fit and honing their personal skills as well as team cohesion, proficiency and dynamics. Soldiers train on assault courses, fast boats, bridges, computers, parade squares, firing ranges, mock-up towns and residential compounds. They rehearse emplaning drills on helicopters and aircraft then abseil or jump out of them. Soldiers camp, cook, clean, read maps and repair themselves as well as their equipment. They learn to survive, to hide and to drive every kind of vehicle in convoys. Soldiers make both plans and life or death decisions. They communicate across metres and miles with sign language and code. The Army stands in when civilian services strike and are the last resort when all else fails. Soldiers think fast, learning to trust themselves and each other; they then put that trust into practice. They repeat packing their kit and checking and cleaning every life-saving item over and over, till it becomes second nature and an extension of themselves. They can quickly put their hand on exactly the right piece of equipment just when they need it, then use it, clean it and repack it. Soldiers learn to watch and wait, to fight and to kill. When they have mastered all of this they learn to do it silently, in the dark, in the snow, the jungle or the desert, when cold, wet, exhausted, in pain and scared.

This is what the Army does.

Acknowledgements

Lighting the Fuse would not have been possible without the help and support of so many people. I owe a debt that I can never repay to my amazing parents who I put through a lot; they have stood by me through thick and thin. I must also thank my mother for giving me my first diary when I was thirteen and encouraging me to keep on writing it; without over forty years of diaries this book would not have been possible. Deepest thanks to my wonderful children, Alexander and Ellen, who have left me in peace to write. To my siblings for being there, always. To my first 'proper' boyfriend Tony, now in Australia, who provided honest opinion and helpful guidance, despite not having seen or spoken to me in over forty years.

An enormous thank you to the hugely supportive Cambridge crew: Karen Ottewell, the wider ceremonial team and the amazing Constabulary who have endured my bright ideas with patience. A special thank you to both Katy Quail and Tim Milner for keeping me on the straight and narrow.

Thanks to Kate Boxell who took the first brave step and handed me the baton to run my race. Huge appreciation is due to those friends, both civilian and military, who read chapters for me, checked their Sandhurst diaries, helped me understand the civilian level of military knowledge (woeful in my opinion) and pointed out the numerous errors; Pridge, Ruth, Jill, Hils, Baby Bernie, Liz and Glamorous Jo. Thanks to the marvellous Sandhurst Sisterhood who provided historical and up-to-date details, as well as a view into today's Army from a female perspective.

Grateful thanks, too, to my agent Lauren Gardner, who not only convinced me to write my story but came up with the brilliant title too. Thanks also to my editors; Emily Barrett who saw the potential and Ru Merritt who ran with it so brilliantly.

Apologies to all those (you know who you are) who featured in any of my wilder adventures but who didn't make it into this book for legal, security or embarrassment reasons. I hope you aren't too disappointed that our magnificent achievements are not included here.

Thanks to *Zebu*, now a heritage ship, and my fellow Venturers who sparked something in me all those years ago, teaching me that I was capable of more.

I also owe a huge debt to all the fabulous women of WSC 891, without whom the adventure would not have happened and this book would never have been written.

Credits

Trapeze would like to thank everyone at Orion who worked on the publication of *Lighting the Fuse*.

Agent
Lauren Gardner

Editor
Ru Merritt

Copy-editor
Tony Hirst

Proofreader
Liz Marvin

Editorial Management
Sarah Fortune
Charlie Panayiotou
Jane Hughes
Claire Boyle

Audio
Paul Stark
Amber Bates

Contracts
Anne Goddard
Jake Alderson

Design
Debbie Holmes
Joanna Ridley
Nick May

Marketing
Yadira Da Trinidade

Publicity
Alainna Hadjigeorgiou

Help us make the next generation of readers

We – both author and publisher – hope you enjoyed this book. We believe that you can become a reader at any time in your life, but we'd love your help to give the next generation a head start.

Did you know that 9 per cent of children don't have a book of their own in their home, rising to 13 per cent in disadvantaged families*? We'd like to try to change that by asking you to consider the role you could play in helping to build readers of the future.

We'd love you to think of sharing, borrowing, reading, buying or talking about a book with a child in your life and spreading the love of reading. We want to make sure the next generation continue to have access to books, wherever they come from.

And if you would like to consider donating to charities that help fund literacy projects, find out more at **www.literacytrust.org.uk** and **www.booktrust.org.uk**.

THANK YOU

*As reported by the National Literacy Trust